Death as related ...

This book is simply one man's attempt at
communication with those of his fellow men
who like to discuss and reflect together. It
presents the thoughts of a man who is deeply
influenced by his medical and psychological
education, by his Christian faith, and by his
priestly commitment.

other persons provides
opportunity to speak
nce. Here, Dr. Oraison
d psychological knowl-
kes a real contribution
cience on death as it
isplantation and other
s.

DEATH—AND THEN WHAT? looks at its subject in three ways: as a personal adventure,
as related to other persons, and as an event
with significance for the Christian.

/HAT? concludes with
er with regard to death.
son says, assumes and
central pivot of every
ng the very center of

The author investigates the personal element
of death as an event which is completely
natural. From his unique, medical-psycholog-
ical point of view Dr. Oraison makes a significant contribution to our understanding of
the meaning of "natural."

sus' violent death and
ected with it—death
e capital event which
mpletes each one of
ive.

Not only is death completely natural, it is
also an event which will happen to everyone.
The chapter entitled "My Death and Me" attempts to demythologize this adventure. These
reflections on the personal aspect of death
conclude with a treatment of suicide.

or of Medicine who
age of 34. He subse-
orate in Theology.
oks are **Learning to**
dvice for teenagers,

and **Love or Constraint,** a contribution to
meaningful parent-child dialogue. Both are
published by Paulist Press.

DEATH—
AND THEN WHAT?

Death—
And Then What?

by
Marc Oraison

Translated by
Theodore DuBois

NEWMAN PRESS
Paramus, N. J.   New York, N. Y.
Amsterdam   Toronto   London

A Newman Press Edition, originally published under the title *La mort . . . et puis apres?* by Librairie Arthème Fayard, Paris, France.

Library of Congress
Catalog Card Number: 73-88522

Published by Newman Press
Editorial Office: 304 W. 58th St., N. Y., N. Y. 10019
Business Office: Paramus, New Jersey 07652

Printed and bound in the
United States of America

Contents

Preface

This book makes no pretense at being a doctrinal treatise; nor is it a philosophical work, since the author is not a philosopher. It is simply one man's attempt at communication with those of his fellow men who like to discuss and reflect together, the thoughts of a man who is deeply influenced by his medical and psychological education, by his Christian faith and by his priestly commitment.

Some readers may be surprised not to find, at the very beginning and throughout the greater part of these pages, an explicit affirmation of the thought of a believer with regard to death. This method of writing is intentional, undoubtedly debatable, but nevertheless deliberately chosen. It has been considered the more fruitful way to express as much as possible the reflections of a modern-day man without drawing upon the enlightenment which the Christian faith brings to death. The intent of this attitude is simple: I want every person who reads this book to feel himself capable of walking along, without being too embarrassed *a priori,* in the company of the author, who is attempting to think about this essential problem by means of merely *human* reflection. In this way, the final explanation of the Christian faith, purposely condensed into a few themes, can be regarded by each person according to his own attitude, without this faith appearing to be an erroneous phenomenon and without its possible intrusion into the fact as humanly lived. Obviously, the Christian apprehension of death is also a fact and cannot be situated as an epiphenomenon. However, it seemed more profitable to develop especially what a believer and an unbeliever can exchange of what is commonly perceived or directly communicable.

Can we reflect validly on a reality that is of the deepest possible concern to us? Can we, without constantly asking ourselves to what degree we are polarizing the discussion by its own affectivity and option, risk some illumination on life, love or sexuality? Can we *really* do so in regard to death, even though we speak and write about it?

On the threshold of this volume, in all honesty—that is, with complete awareness of the possibility of involuntary and inexorable dishonesty—the author poses this question, but without offering an exhaustive reply. In a sense both of us are embarking on an adventure.

Medical experience plays an important role here, because it is nothing but "scientific." The medical student who is just beginning work on anatomical complexities smokes a pipe—because of the smell?—and juggles "pieces of meat" when cadavers are available for dissection. Only many years later will he be able to admit that this was the only way he could defend himself against an obscure and fundamental agony. This inert, stunted form inevitably evokes the brutal perception of his own finitude.

The experience of what life is in certain sectors of the world also causes a person to reflect. We see an anomalous multitude literally swarming around us—young girls and boys, needy workers, curious onlookers, tourists, revellers, etc. We perceive so many anxious looks whose terror pierces through, more or less, from under their smiles, or explodes around a corner like a tragic call. And each one of these looks betrays a consciousness which questions itself, and which, clearly or not, poses to itself, as it does to me, the question of *its* destiny. From the squalor of the inner city to the tree-lined suburbs, under such different appearances, we find the same agony and the same misery of consciousness struggling with time— that is, with the "end."

Beyond this somewhat theatrical tragic stage of whimpering sentimentality and bitter irony, where can we situate reflection that will be humble, accepting, lived and not abstract? Without doubt, in line with a humor whose laughter is mixed with tears. An English humorist wrote: "Do not take life *too* seriously; you will not leave it alive." This is a strangely profound sentence, because in this "advice" there is not a suggestion of being careless, but rather of not being *too* serious —that is, of having a sense of the relative value of life in time. On the other hand, we do "leave it," and the least we can say is that we do not leave it "alive," for the moment we leave it means that we are. . . .

In a very different style, this recalls a formula written by St. Augustine: "Whenever you do anything, do it as if the world's destiny depended on it, and at the same time as if you were to die the minute afterward and it had no importance."

Before proceeding, the author asks the one who is beginning this book to savor the richness and convergence of these aphorisms. And then he begs the reader not to forget that, in embarking on this voyage on the subject of death, the author's concern is as great as his own; both of us are united in the fraternity of a question that is both personal and common.

And as an introductory paradox, we can agree to this unexpected definition heavy with meaning: "Death? A regrettable loss of time."

CHAPTER ONE

Death Is Completely Natural

"I can't bear," said Mrs. Bouton as she ate her oysters, "the fact that we make animals suffer by killing them. It's intolerable! Take the bullfights, for example. . . ."

By then she was on her ninth oyster, which she devoured contentedly with a well-placed bite into its pulpy flesh.

Some of her friends thought: "She's an oyster," which is a manner of speaking, certainly, and means quite simply that between the cerebral system of Mrs. Bouton and the nervous organization of this mollusk, there was not a very great difference, at least at first sight.

Then, because it was around Christmas, turkey with chestnut stuffing was brought to the table and skillfully carved by the headwaiter, who put the head aside for the gourmets.

Launched on a subject that quite visibly was close to her heart, Mrs. Bouton moved from the bloody arenas to Hindu philosophy, and marveled that Buddha respected life to the point that they say he delicately picked up the flea that was bothering him and, careful not to cause it the least harm, placed it on the ground. She had read this in a book. . . . And all during her conversation, she relished like a true gourmet the aromatic delicacy of the turkey wing that was her portion.

Some of those in her circle said of Mrs. Bouton: "She's a good person, but, just between us, she's a turkey"—this, of course, being more complimentary, since the cerebral system of this ample bird is quite a bit more developed than that of the previously mentioned mollusk.

Then they began to talk politics, and Mrs. Bouton re-
joiced enthusiastically over the massacres which are defending
civilization so nobly in Vietnam. . . .

But this leads to another kind of reflection.

Without going in search of complicated paradoxes, it
suffices to consider the turkey which lived, grew and prospered
in such a way that it could be offered to diners. It accom-
plished this by pecking at seeds and digesting them—seeds
which, had it not been for the turkey, might have germinated,
grown and given forth splendid ears of corn, which in turn.
. . . In other words, on the level of the turkey, it is in destroying
vegetable life that animal life can prosper. Furthermore,
vegetable life itself could not have developed except by drawing its resources from a very complex magma which we call
earth and which has been—although we seldom think of it—
since the time when all these processes began, the residue, the
thick soup of an infinite variety of dead things.

The turkey is therefore the product of a multitude of dead
things. And it in turn was killed and put in the oven for the
sole purpose of enabling Mrs. Bouton and her dinner companions to live, to speak and even to think according to the
level of their intellectual development.

If the diners did not eat, it is quite evident that after a
certain time they would wither away and cease to live. Death
by inanition is one of the clinical forms of death, rare or
frequent according to the times or the geographical region.
But in eating to live, the diners maintain a process that is
complex and truly contradictory: they satiate themselves—in
different ways, according to their manner of life—they grow
old and they die.

This leads us to formulate a proposition which at first sight
is paradoxical, but which in fact is nothing but a first truth,
as well as an enormous banality: it is death which makes
things live, and it is life which makes things die. In this regard
we mean the death of other things, generally, and one's own
life (independent of the cases where others kill you in order

to live, which, indeed, is generally the official reason for wars).

Current language expresses this very well. When we lose an aged parent, some people say to us: "It's unfortunate, but that's life," which tends to say, after all, that life is death, albeit with a certain delay. Definitely, the most universally natural thing in life is death.

Meanwhile, from the protozoan to the creative genius of a Michelangelo, a Bach, a Pasteur or an Einstein, there took place this curious phenomenon, difficult to situate historically speaking: that there have been living beings who have attained sufficient cerebral development to be able to perceive the fact of death and to think about it, and that after all their reflection they do not agree in their conclusions; they do not find it "natural" at all. In other words, they *suffer* from it.

Since we are very accustomed to it, life seems very simple at first sight. From so-called inert matter, it bursts forth on every side, in every direction, with an exuberance which approaches disorder, and yet with a rigorous, dynamic order which results in the fact that a grain of wheat will never grow into a pumpkin plant, for example, but always into a stalk of wheat (unless man sticks his nose into the matter, because we do not know all that he is capable of—but we will discuss this later—).

Modern science is showing us how life is much more complex, incomprehensible and awesome than we had believed, and how, at the same time, it remains in continuity with what is not "living." Molecular biology is a recent science, and modern genetics, as well as bio-chemistry, has discovered molecular structures specific to "living matter." However, we will not go into detail on this, since it would require extensive knowledge of a subject in which I am not well versed and of whose existence few of my readers are even aware.

I think that we can express the results of these extremely complex findings in the following manner. What we call life is undoubtedly nothing but the emergence of a certain type of molecular arrangement. But this arrangement attains a structuration whose complexity is stupefying—and much more so on the level of bio-chemistry than on the more easily observable level of anatomy and physiology.

The observable characteristic of this awesome molecular structuration is its very caducity. Aging and death are specific to living structure. Biologically, death is the natural result of life.

Even if we pretend to regard the fact as normal, it is rather extraordinary to think that matter has been organizing itself for billions of centuries to make it possible—we do not know how—for you and me, each independently, to live, feel, speak, love and cry, and, finally, for each of us, as we say, to breathe "his last" unwillingly—all of that activity only to end up in man's protesting against a situation which, at first sight, cannot have any different outcome.

What, then, happens on the level of "consciousness of life" —and therefore of death—which is the specific characteristic of the human race?

Let us also note in passing that two questions remain posed and without answers (since it is proper to man to pose questions, I see no reason for embarrassment): (1) Why do things happen in this way? (2) Can't we conceive that this living structuration might attain the level of the definitive by means of some kind of "new mutation," truly unimaginable, but the hypothesis of which we cannot rationally reject *a priori?*

For the moment, therefore, and according to what observation permits us to know, we may say that death is as "natural" to life as is life itself. But what do we mean by "natural"? It will undoubtedly be useful to stop for a minute to discuss this point, a very controversial one at the present time.

These present discussions are not "sophisms" or escapes. What popular language until recent years understood by "nature" (in reference to morality, for example) corresponds to the ideas we could have had before knowing how things in the world really happen—that is, before the development of scientific knowledge in the proper sense of the term. However, it is quite clear that this no longer harmonizes with the concept which modern man can have of the world, of himself, and of himself in the world.

But reflection on this level is delicate. Criticizing the notion of nature which is the vehicle for traditional thought is not equivalent to rejecting it as false. It would be somewhat naive to believe that men were incapable of thought until our times! Refusal to modify our thought and to enrich it, as we are constrained to do by the advent of science, would be an error no less serious. It really seems that these are the two errors inherent in the present effort of reflection.

Words have their importance, especially those whose frequent and varied use results in harmful equivocations. This is true of the words "nature" and "natural." On the one hand we say that certain conduct is "contrary to nature," and on the other hand we deny any philosophical foundation to the notion of "nature" understood in this way. And yet this word, like any other, must correspond to something. It would be useful, perhaps, to reflect on what it means by taking immediate experience, systematically and exclusively, as a point of departure.

When I say, "That is natural," and I want to confirm my thought and make it more precise, I add, "That is self-evident." In other words, the "that" of which I am speaking appears, propels and expresses itself, unfolds, acts, by a dynamism interior to it and in which nothing exterior intervenes. If it is a matter of logical reasoning, for example, it is only its proper application which is in question. It can happen that I may make a mistake and that my reasoning may be false, but this changes nothing in the development of its proper dynamism. If it is a matter of someone's conduct, the idea is basically the same: Gertrude gives birth to a nice baby boy who was very much waited for; she and her husband rejoice; it is "natural," it is "self-evident," and nothing exterior to it opposes the dynamic unfolding of the event.

But if the baby immediately vomits everything given to him, this is no longer "natural"; the doctor is called, and he performs a stenosis of the pylorus so that things may once again be "natural." This introduces us to the first meaning of the word "nature": what observation shows us of the world and of its movement.

Before going further, it will be useful to mention that it is we who speak of "nature," and not the universe which surrounds us. "Nature" is a word, and therefore an idea developed from phantasms (in the Thomistic as well as in the Freudian sense)—that is, a human interpretation. This does not deny the value or meaning of the word or of the idea; it is merely necessary not to lose sight of the fact that the idea of nature is always subjective and relative and does not adequately correspond to the reality of it which we can grasp in no other way than by meditating on our experience.

A first meaning of the word "natural" corresponds to "what happens so long as man does not intervene by his thought and action." I look at a brook flowing down a mountainside; its course is natural, and I rejoice at its freshness. If I construct a dam of stones, nothing is any longer "natural"; I introduce into "nature," into what is happening, something artificial. But if, while I look without acting, something happens on the desert mountain—a landslide, for example—and I see that the brook has stopped flowing, I will be tempted to say that this is not "natural," and I will ask myself who did such a good job of closing the faucet. Here, the word "natural" designates *that to which I am accustomed* and which satisfies me in different ways. The primitive meaning is modified because the landslide which occurred on the mountain is a natural phenomenon; in our hypothesis, human intervention had nothing to do with it. Therefore, I must be careful before making a definitive judgment; things which do not appear to me to be natural can happen in nature. What, then, is *truly* natural? I must recognize that I can never have a definitive and completely exhaustive answer to this question.

On the banks of my brook are fields where thistles are

growing wild. If I watch them long enough, I will see the wind disperse their seeds and the field become covered with thistles with no place for any other vegetation. This is natural, even though I may tend to think that it would be just as "natural" for the summer flowers "to have a right" to grow as well and not be suffocated and overcome by these "dirty thistles." On seeing this, I begin to work. I plow the field (which presupposes a certain number of preliminary operations: the discovery of iron, the invention of the plow and the domestication and use of animals). I plant fresh new grass which, vigorous and strong, does away with the thistles. I thus avenge the flowers of the field, and I will have good grazing for my animals, provided that they do not eat the grass while it is budding. All of this is no longer "natural"; it is artificial in the proper sense of the term—and it is very complicated because I have "contradicted nature" in killing earthworms, larvae, the thistles and many other little insects and forms of plant life in order to "favor nature" by making life possible for the grass, for my cows, and even for myself, since I like butter.

Without any question, don't I have a tendency to designate as nature whatever favors and satisfies me? And what is the weight of culture in all of this? Why is it natural to eat fried cockroaches in one geographical latitude, whereas in another this would be looked upon as an aberration?

This favorable interpretation of benevolent nature leads to the touching naiveté of a Bernardin de Saint Pierre who writes: "There is no less convenience in the forms and sizes of fruits. There are many which are tailored for man's mouth, like the cherries and plums; others for his hand, like the pears and apples; others, much larger, like the melons, are divided on their sides, as if destined to be eaten by a family" (*Etudes de la Nature*).

If we hold to the observation of what happens so long as man does not intervene, "nature" seems to be both singularly oriented and curiously incoherent, marked by the promotion of life and destructive riot, the bursting forth of existence and

continual crumbling, structurations pushed high and fundamental fragility. Death is as "natural" as life, whether it
results from internal or external factors.

The moment that man intervenes, everything changes.
Man acts on what he finds and introduces to it a new dimension which I propose to call "art" or "artifice." Some call this
"culture," because man's "nature" seems to be, precisely,
"culture."

But this "culture"—in the most general sense of the term—
is always exercised on a pre-existing "nature," however imprecise it may be. The difficult thing to make precise is the
articulation of these two factors. From this viewpoint, modern
science has profoundly modified the ideas which we had of
them up until now. The margin of "culture" seems much more
vast than it did formerly (and this, moreover, contains an
implicit affirmation of human freedom, certitude and responsibility—and, therefore, of agony). One of the most striking
aspects of this upheaval is underlined by knowledge of the
physiological and psychological aspects of sexuality, but there
nevertheless remains something irreducible. When certain
philosophers carry on a discussion for hours to show that
"nature" does not exist, the idea sometimes comes to me to
be patient, to wait until their kidneys have filled their bladders
and, on the level of their conscious perception, there occurs
the complex phenomenon commonly referred to as "the need
to urinate," and then to ask them if they think that this phenomenon—humiliating to pure intellectuals—comes from
"nature" or from "culture."

In any case, it is proper to man to intervene. But we
should be sure to recognize that this intervention is very
contradictory. It goes from the invention of aspirin to the
invention of the atomic bomb. The progress of science in
performing appendectomies has saved hundreds of thousands
of lives, but advances in the automobile industry, somewhat
contemporary, have had quite the reverse effect on society.
Besides, we have to recognize the fact that the persons who
were saved by this progress in surgery have ended up dying

from something else—and not necessarily from an automobile accident.

To complete, to better "nature," around oneself and in oneself: this, in principle, is the meaning of culture—that is, the "nature" of man. It consists in contradicting what would happen spontaneously; this is why we shave and cut our nails, things which, in a way, could be qualified as "anti-natural." But it also consists in inventing the fabulous product which will maintain a head of hair or make it grow back again, or replace what is lacking, such as a leg, which we then call "artificial," or fight against inevitable aging to "repair the irreparable outrage of time."

Since the time of Noah, "culture" of the vine has certainly made great progress, as have the processes of winemaking or distillation. It furnishes us with the experience of the incomparable taste of a great Médoc or of a royal Armagnac artfully aged, but it also furnishes, necessarily by the same channel but for infinitely more complex motives, cirrhosis of the liver or delirium tremens. And the seemingly ridiculous fact of the matter is that the prudent drinker, anxious not to become an alcoholic, will perhaps die at the age of forty from pulmonary congestion, whereas the impenitent drinker will down eight quarts per day, survive repeated bouts of drunkenness, and die at the age of eighty-five in an accident.

In one way or another, by "aberration" or by weakness, "culture"—man's nature—ends up in death. I cannot remember which lucid author wrote, "We recover from every illness except the last one"—evidence which it is not always easy to accept, at least for oneself, or in a philosophical system that would like to disown it.

In another perspective, however, it is useful to notice that this is really a happy situation. If we did not die, life would soon become impossible.

I think that there is in this another camouflaged piece of evidence, a fundamental contradiction, as blind as the one which pushes us to increase unceasingly the number and speed of automobiles, while traffic, because of that very fact, becomes more and more difficult and murderous. I mean that we eagerly dream of the time when man will have conquered aging and death, without taking account of the fact that, when that happens, hatred and reciprocal massacre will be the only solution to the resultant overpopulation. It is curious that, on one hand, we dream of prolonging life, even indefinitely, while on the other hand, to remove the specter of intolerable overpopulation, we quite readily work to advance the cause of birth control. But, for a great part of the human population, what is life without the joys of fatherhood and motherhood? To admit the idea of a world in which we would no longer die, we must first of all suppress not only sexual fecundity, but also the desire for this fecundity. Such an idea can only make us smile; it demands the naiveté of "a bedroom philosopher," the clinical psychologist who believes he can solve the affective complexity of human beings, beginning with his own, merely by a series of questions which he considers relevant.

In 1957, with Plon, Michel Carrouges published a very interesting novel entitled *Les grands-pères prodiges* (The Prodigious Grandfathers). In a kind of "science fiction" style, but one which expresses very profound thought (on about the same level as Vercors' *Les animaux dénaturés*), he describes a scientific discovery capable of making old people young almost indefinitely.

One of the characters in this book speaks explicitly of "the catastrophic postponement of mortality." He shows that even if we could solve the problem of nourishment, the overpopulation destined to follow, in a greater or lesser length of time, would end up being intolerable: "Men will be so tightly packed, one against the other, that they will die of tedium."

If we are willing to be wary of nonsense, as he wants us to be, we must agree on this matter, the apparent paradox of which is heavy with a truth difficult to bear: for a world without death to be livable, it would be necessary that no one else be born and that, at least for a time, each one find his age arrested at the point he had attained—and this would have to be true universally. In other words, it would be necessary to resolve and empty out the contradiction of time, and this is equivalent to killing desire (or, in other words, life) by remaining at a point of dissatisfaction without the least opening for *possible* hope.

However we take it, death appears to be the *natural* factor most important to the living phenomenon, the factor which makes this phenomenon possible, which enables it to perpetuate itself *in time,* and which, on the level of man, enables it, precisely, to live in the dynamism of his desire and in "hope" for a solution. It is not at all ridiculous to say that it is because we die that we live.

Since we are speaking of "nature" in the sense in which scientific knowledge obliges us to deepen our reflection, it would be a mistake to pass over in silence what we learn about ourselves from psychoanalysis, inasmuch as it is an investigation of our proper, lived reality. We will return to it in greater detail later, but it will be useful to underline immediately the fact that affective human experience, such as occurs, is inscribed essentially in a dialectic of time and death. It is itself the stimulant, and it would be naive to draw from it some kind of hasty "pessimism" (which can be quickly qualified as masochistic) or to flee this dialectic in some kind of idealistic "optimism" (which can be quickly qualified as childish).

"Man's nature" is to be "outside of nature," but without knowing where he is going. It is to have a progressive consciousness of himself as a subject, but a consciousness that is simultaneously menaced, by his very condition of duration (in the sense of time *lived*), with being annihilated *as such.*

Man's nature is agony.

But does this mean a blind alley?

From any viewpoint, modern science does not permit us to affirm that it does. I think that this fact is not without importance.

CHAPTER TWO

My Death and Me

Strictly speaking, death does not exist. There is not a "thing" or a mysterious person called "death." It seems to me important to emphasize this and not to lose sight of it. Indeed, we could otherwise end up feeling that we are up against an enemy as vague as it is certain, with whom we are fighting and who ends up by overcoming us. This is the usual mythical and iconographical representation, with the silhouette of a skeleton more or less draped and armed with a scythe, a figure very prominent during certain centuries.

But this line of perception and perspective, even though it is undeniably poetic, leads to a dead end in every way, or, more exactly, to a way of formulating the incomprehensible— or the mystery—in a manner that is actually unacceptable. To make a comparison, I will say that a child can attribute a sort of fabulous personality to the moon, whereas an adult can conceive of it only as an element in a very complex system. This does not make it any easier for the adult to answer the questions which this implies, but at least the problem is better posed. It is no longer "What is the moon, and what does it want of me?" but rather "What is the meaning of the system of which it is a part?" And if there is thought beyond this system, we can no longer conceive of it in the mythological mode.

The same is true of death. It is not an "existing entity." What exists is we, who die. Death is exclusively a fact, and,

16

more precisely, a fact which happens to us; it is, as we say, *a personal event.*

This is the reason for the title of this chapter. Not that I intend to give myself over to affective or spiritual effusions with regard to my own reaction in the face of death. But it seems to me of capital importance to indicate forcefully that death is nothing but a personal event in someone's history. It happens that we are all concerned with this event, and from this results a choice of language related to St. Paul's words in Romans 7 ("I do not do the good I want") or to the thought of certain modern philosophers called phenomenologists. This means—it seems to me—that if my death is an adventure which happens to me, it is also an adventure which happens to whoever is doing me the honor of reading this book. It will be lived by him in a way that is strictly incommunicable, but we can, he and I, say "I"—and say it to each other. Death is an event in his history as it is in mine—and it is nothing else.

What the meaning of this event is for me is another question! But it is necessary first of all to "demythologize" it or risk dizziness and fear. It is useless to hide the fact that the myth is, in a way, reassuring. It gives one the illusion of being in command of the situation.

This event of my death, when I look at it closely enough, is of a banality that needs no commentary. First of all, it is an event that is common to all of us, without any possible exception. And we have seen that it is, in a way, constitutive, much more than "fatal." In fact, the only other event in my history which presents the same character is my birth—and this is linked with "biological time" itself.

Growth—in the broadest sense of the word—is also a constitutive event in its successive stages; it is, after all, birth, life and death. But each of these stages or each of these indicative manifestations is in fact contingent. A particular individual may not achieve "the state of puberty" for various pathological reasons, but may attain the size and weight of an adult individual. Even this event, as important to someone's history as is psychosomatic adolescence, might not happen, and it will immediately be felt that this is very "abnormal."

In another perspective, less directly biological, we can say that all of the historical events in someone's existence are more or less highly probable beforehand, but that no single one is absolutely certain beforehand. This is true not only with regard to the moment, but with regard to the fact itself.

We can find many examples. I have begun to write this book, but it is not *certain* that I will complete it or that my intention will persist. A certain young man intends to marry and to have a home with a certain young woman, but he is not *certain* that this will happen; engagements have been "broken" the night before the ceremony.

In summary, everything in the life of a human being is nothing but intention; its realization is always uncertain. Besides, the border between the "dream" and the "intention" is always an imprecise one, as neat as it may seem, even in terms of this incertitude.

Birth and death alone have this character of absolute certitude. But whereas birth can be located in time as something acquired, death cannot be. And my situation in relation to this event of my life is strictly the inverse of my situation in relation to all others. Right now I am planning to make a trip to Europe in three months; if I want to be honest, I must recognize that although all the arrangements have been made, something can still "go wrong" to prevent it, which would *annul* this "more than probable" and nevertheless uncertain event. On the other hand, I can have no idea of the moment of my death, but I am *certain* that it will happen. And it is the only event in my life for which my certitude is reversed, bearing on the fact and not on the date.

The uncertainty of the fact—like my trip to Europe—eventually gives rise to impatience. But uncertainty with regard to the date of a fact that is certain gives rise, rather, to agony, especially since death is an event which, strictly speaking, is at the same time unexplorable. It is, first of all, absolutely different from any other experience which I can have—that is, there is no point of reference in my experience that can serve to give me the least idea of it. For every other event in my life —including the death of the person dearest to me—I can make use of analogies which enable me to prepare for it, even unconsciously, but for my death there is nothing. Nothing analogous to it has happened in my life (except, perhaps, my birth—but I know nothing about that either; we will return to this point later).

Personally, I have not yet had occasion to "have a brush with death," as they say, because of an accident or a serious illness. But it seems to me that this experience in someone's existence cannot serve to explore the event of death, properly speaking, for the very simple reason that, precisely, *the person is not dead*. At most, the person has felt his temporality, his caducity. "How little we are, after all!" say the philosophers. But that only shows one side, the one we can already know without their help if only we reflect a little. Persons who have had experiences of this kind retain hardly more than this impression, more or less clearly assumed, or are engulfed in the black hole of amnesia—which does not fail to be worrisome. "I do not remember anything after the moment that the car came toward us, and they tell me that I did not regain consciousness until three days after the accident." A relatively banal sentence—but what does "regain consciousness" mean? What happened during the "intervening time"? No one knows or can say anything about it, but in any case it has nothing to do with death, precisely because it is the "intervening time." And what can be signified by or result from the fact that, in circumstances of this kind, the person cannot be aware of what happened during that time except through the testimony of others?

Nor does sleep offer any elements for analogy. Strictly speaking, the expression "to sleep his last sleep" is completely absurd, and perhaps expresses nothing more than a conscious or implicit hope for some kind of "awakening." But, precisely, an essential element of sleep is that we awaken from it; in other words, it is still a matter of duration. We cannot have conscious experience of sleep, and therefore we cannot say what occurs during it, because it is by definition the suspension of consciousness which permits the irruption of the dream, the symbolic expression of unconscious life. But it is lived as *duration*—that is, in terms of an explorable "afterward." When I go to sleep at night, I "put aside" the projects which I have planned for the following day and whose realization I have more or less imagined. However, I have absolutely nothing at all which permits me to *imagine* the "afterward" of the event of capital importance which is my death; nothing permits me even to affirm or deny a possible "afterward" in the same mode as any other event. No experience already lived truly authorizes me to do so, except, perhaps the elementary evidence that an event, by definition, has a "sequel." Contrary to all the other probable events in my life, for that one, which is certain, this elementary evidence is itself without practical consequence.

Strictly speaking, I should say that I cannot *speak* of my death *as an event,* although it is such, and among the more "massive" ones. In April 1966, Paul Ricoeur declared: "I cannot speak of an event if it is only a rupture; I speak of it to the degree in which, setting out from this event, I can assemble suspended significations. Suppose that it is an event like the taking of the Bastille: the raw event is nothing as long as I am not in a state, from that point on, to bind together everything which was being prepared in the currents of thought of the 18th century, in the people's demands, etc.; likewise, the event is such to the degree that it opens up perspectives, that it begins new series of other events connected between themselves and capable of being understood in their connection. Consequently, there can be an event only by the assembly of meaning before and after the event."

But, contrary to the taking of the Bastille, my death concerns me directly. I can apprehend the events which prepare it, and I can grasp its certitude—in uncertainty with regard to its date—but I cannot go any farther, for I find myself up against the unexplorable, the *apparently* nonsensical. In speaking of my death, I cannot speak of a fact, because it is an event which concerns me; but neither can I speak of it as an event, because, as Ricoeur says, I cannot explore "behind" it. Nothing embarrasses me as much as my death!

This leads us to a rather paradoxical conclusion: when I speak of my death or when I think about it, I affirm myself in a particularly peremptory way as existing. It is even the ultimate circumstance which enables me to perceive that I can in no way conceive of myself as "non-existing." From the moment that *I* conceive of *myself, I am,* both as subject and object of my thought. If "I conceive of myself as dead," it is the object alone which has changed appearance, but, if we may say so, the subject is thereby only all the more affirmed.

More exactly, I should say that it is impossible for me to *conceive* of myself as dead. At most, I can *imagine* myself as such. But if we look closely, it is still illusory. What I imagine is my agony or my corpse which *I* look at in my imagination, but not at all "my no longer existing." In fact, it is radically impossible for me to imagine that I no longer am, since, precisely, I am when I imagine. I can *imagine* that I no longer *exist;* I cannot *imagine* that I no longer *am.*

This contradiction is troubling enough. I know that I will die, but I cannot apprehend this fact as an event, as Ricoeur says; in no way can I apprehend it as a *non-being of "me."*

Moreover, when I imagine my death or burial, it is always in terms of the public, the *other* person(s)— singular or plural —and of the effect which it will have on the spectator. I think that this experience is universal. "But when I'm dead, then you'll be sorry!"

And I imagine to myself, with more or less pleasure, the persons standing around, or others who will then be obliged to recognize the merits that I had and the importance which I incarnated. It is then they will feel the "loss"! I do not believe that, when we think of our own death, we can imagine that the others might finally be glad to be rid of us. Or, in a subtle way, we imagine that this impression of "good riddance" will be particularly embarrassing to them, and basically culpable. If, in thought, I see anyone as "well rid" of me by my death, it is because I anticipate that it will make them uneasy to feel that way and that somehow I will avenge myself for a lack of understanding from which I *presently* suffer.

But there arises another aspect in this. When I imagine others looking at my death—or when I imagine my death in the presence of others, which amounts to the same thing—this means that I become "he-who-sees-without-being-seen." I assist at the scene of my burial, for example, and I see the persons who are looking at my corpse or at my casket. But it is elementary and primordial that from that moment I situate myself as looking at other persons who do not see me looking at them and who see of me nothing but a residue without consistency. They can no longer truly apprehend me; they *no longer know where I am;* I have become invisible, but I can see.

This joins us directly to the dialectic of looking, which is so fundamental to the development of a subject's consciousness, according to psychoanalytical data. To see without being seen—as if it were "culpable" or "dangerous" to be seen seeing. In a certain sense, in imagining others in the presence of my death, I "realize" the old dream of the ring of Gigès.

This means that I can think of my death—or even simply of myself—only in terms of what someone else sees. But this also means that in order to overcome and resolve this fundamental dialectic of the agony of the look, I must, by means of my imagination, situate myself in a state other than that of time. And this is in itself impossible, since I can imagine myself only in time.

There is something in this which makes me think of the desperate efforts of a prisoner to break his chains. He *knows* that freedom exists, but he cannot attain it. His efforts are oriented toward the real, and are simultaneously unreal.

In any case, the "prisoner of time" which I am cannot imagine himself as "non-being," and he who declares that he is not afraid of death because "there is nothing afterward" is fooling himself and reassuring himself cheaply by emptying the problem. This is what the child does who denies what he is afraid of. My death is therefore for me the certain fact in my own history which I can in no way explore.

At the other end of myself, I also plunge into the unexplorable. I have no "memory" of my birth, of my first meetings with these people who are not me and who surround me. And yet, all of this is somehow inscribed in the primitive structuration of myself which constitutes me, and which underlies me not only chronologically but continually, "from bottom to top," and which is commonly called the unconscious. Nevertheless, since the time of my birth (and even before my birth) other persons knew me, while I was still unable to perceive myself and to disengage my own consciousness of myself. They knew me, albeit with a huge margin of uncertainty as to what I would later become, but it took me a long time to know myself—that is, to know that I am me, and that I am the only one who is me. This process took many years, during which I was obliged to depend on what others told me. My mother told me that I began to speak in a somewhat comprehensible way at about two years of age. I certainly want to believe it—because I have no other way of knowing it.

It does, after all, make me rather dizzy: "I," in my identity, my solitude and my ever evolving relations, navigate through time between two unexplorables. This contrasts almost intolerably with the sentiment which I have to exist, my radical incapability to think of myself as non-being, and my "thirst to know" what the very meaning of my existence is. At the extreme, this leads almost to a revolt. But who is mocked by it?

One day, a man and a woman met. They decided to live together and to "confront" their respective genital powers. Some time later, in the corner of a hollow muscle in my mother, a certain cellular and molecular grouping began to develop—in a parasitical way, that is—already endowed with a certain autonomy. Quickly enough they noticed it, and they

said, "If it's a boy, we'll call him Marc." Voilà. I already
existed; I was already named; I corresponded beforehand to
their image of me and to their desire for me. But I did not
know it—not until much later. There I was, launched on an
adventure—but this means nothing, because I did not exist
beforehand. There I was, *existing* without knowing it, and in
such a way that had I become conscious of myself, I would
have found myself in an integral process with regard to my
own individual beginnings. *I* navigate—in the sense of "voyage"—between my blastular stage and my death. And I cannot
explore anything of one or the other, in this unquestionable
certitude of my being.

And that is what life is.

I did not "ask" to live . . . and I do not ask to die.

If often happens that I, like everyone, make decisions,
interior ones or not, important ones or not. They can be
formulated, for example, in the following way: "The day after
tomorrow, I will do my shopping and I will buy a pair of
shoes"—a banal enough sentence and one that is apparently
of little consequence. But do we notice that, in saying it, we
express a kind of break, a rupture, a really incomprehensible
dialectical reality?

I will do—as we learn in grammar, the verb is in the
"future." This means that it expresses time, the uncompleted,
the "not-yet-acquired." But the pronoun expresses a certain
situation of the subject—that is, of me—which commands
time, rides over it and uses it. The day after tomorrow does
not yet exist, and it remains uncertain, whereas "I" exist and
I assume that I will exist the day after tomorrow. Whether we
want it or not, whether we perceive it or not, this little sentence, which in a way summarizes existence, is both the insertion of the "I" into time and its extratemporality. "I" is
something other than "the day after tomorrow," even though
it is connected with its uncertainty. *And there is no way of
speaking differently.* I spend my time saying that I am *in*
time, but that I am not—without even wanting to.

This is the same thing as saying that I perceive myself more and more in a kind of successive construction of myself, in multiple and diverse relations, conflicting or not, with other "I's." It is in duration—time lived—that I perceive myself, but invincibly as commanding it. I am simultaneously within and on top of it—just as I am in imagining my death.

There is a first consequence which we should note in passing: namely, that man's "nature" is not only to introduce "culture" into the world, but also to be conscious of himself in intention, of which all the acts are indissociable, but discernible, one from the other. If we understand "duration" to mean the time lived by a consciousness, then duration—a consciousness of self in continual becoming and oriented to a certain realization, whatever it may be—is proper to man. When I was young and I tried to understand and retain the branches of the internal maxillary artery—the anatomists' classical trap—it was because I was studying, as we say, *my* medicine. Those grey hours were solid ones for me, despite their present fruitlessness, leading to the triumphal hours during my internship and the occasion when I performed my first appendectomy. In the life of a couple, sexual acts which are infertile because of the choice of times or other means can be virtually fertile in the sense that they give the couple a deeper relationship in view of the fruitful genital act whose fulfillment they foresee when it is humanly possible to them. It seems to me that in this there is a perspective of considerable importance for methodical reflection.

Another consequence, related more directly to our topic, is that "duration," in the sense in which we have defined it (time consciously lived), is *equivalent to* consciousness of death. We return here to the level of biological ascertainment, not perceived in the mode of scientific knowledge, but in what I might dare to call the existential perception of its own biological participation—*personal* and *engaging* perception, of quite another order than an intellectual one. In this, perhaps, consists the fundamental aspect of the crisis of adolescence.

Two observable facts, among others, manifest the mutation

which takes place with regard to the integration of *real* duration. First of all, there is the normal tendency to day-dream, experienced as an incoercible need. The adolescent "dreams of his life," alongside of his real activity, in themes that are personal to him and rooted in all of his affective evolution and education. One sees himself as an explorer, another as a jet pilot, another as a piano virtuoso (while he hardly knows the notes of the scale). In these adolescent dreams, there is always more or less something of a "desire to impose oneself on the world" in a way that has value or is even spectacular. But there is also a characteristic of intemporality, in the sense that the subject who is the hero of the day-dream is in a way fixed to a certain ideal and events unfold for him without really changing him. For the adolescent, on the level of the imaginary, there is already a break between the "I" and activity; the "I" in the dream is imagined as having reached an immobile perfection.

On the other hand, the adolescent finds it difficult to "realize duration" in real relationships. This is very striking among adolescents who live in conditions where it is difficult for them to gain acceptance, like the hippies, for example, because the phenomenon is then pushed to the extreme. On several occasions, I have been involved in a conversation like this:

"Do you have any idea of what you want to become?"

"Well . . . I don't know . . . Maybe a bartender."

"But what do you like to do?"

"I'm interested in electricity."

"Then why don't you try to become an electrician?"

The silence which follows does not signify anything which we can label as laziness—despite our immediate temptation to "moralize"—but rather an insurmountable difficulty to project. The continuation of the conversation well illustrates this:

"If you prefer, I'll ask the question in a different way. You are now seventeen years old; how do you picture yourself in ten years, when you'll be twenty-seven years old?"

At this point something invariably happened which, the first few times, was very surprising to me; the boy reacted as though I had spoken to him in ancient Greek. He did not *understand* the question. In other words, he was not able to grasp it in his own personal duration.

In a very general way, we can say that passage through adolescence consists in access to relations lived with the adult world, but also relations in which the subject seeks to be recognized, "accepted," as an adult. In other words, the subject seeks to engage in real relationships, whereas until then he had lived in a world where play, as a symbolic realization, was dominant. But this insertion into the real human world includes the integration of his own real duration, the perception of himself as growing older and, fundamentally, as "before death." This does not mean that a child cannot think of death, but he does so in another way. Believing it equivalent to a "departure elsewhere," a "disappearance" (and not an annihilation), the child views death in terms of the reaction which he observes in the adults around him. From the time of adolescence, death is seen as a personal event inscribed in one's own duration. In other words, we can say that it is only from the time of adolescence that death concerns us personally with its interrogative signification for the future and with the specificity of certitude and unexplorability about which we have been thinking.

It does not seem that we have to look for any other reason for the "anti-older generation" attitude of adolescents in general. It comes from a defensiveness against duration—that is, against death.

This is also, undoubtedly, the deep reason for the young person's "taste for danger." He feels conscious of his own life when he confronts the menace. He tries to experience, in a way, the fact that he possesses his life, and that he has mastery over it, by surmounting both dangers and fear. This amounts almost to a "denial of death," as paradoxical as this may seem, to an affirmation of oneself as triumphant over the unavoidable menace which results from consciousness of one's own duration.

Finally, my death is irreversible, like my birth. But unlike everything that can happen to me, these two events are radically absolute.

If I have failed in a competitive exam that has an age limit fixed to it, and if my age precludes the possibility of giving it another try, the fact is irreversible, but I can find a compensation for my failure; I can do something else. If I am married and my wife dies, the fact of my loss is irreversible, but I can remarry. The same is true for everything of which we can think. But for my death, there is no compensation, no arrangement; I die, and that is all.

The same is true also for my birth. I live, and that is all. There is no nuance in the dilemma "to be or not to be." My birth and my death are not only irreversible; they are events of massive importance, and the one eventually necessitates the other.

But this amounts to saying that my existence is irreversible. I can neither think of nor imagine my death as a non-being of "I." I perceive my birth, at the other end of the long process of the development of my consciousness, as the irreversible inauguration of my presence to the world and to myself. Logically, I should think of my death as an absolute and irreversible change of my *personal* being, itself irreversible.

In summary, doesn't this correspond to the notion of Greek philosophy about the "immortality of the soul" (except that the dualism underlying Platonic thought is no longer acceptable to modern thought, and the language itself capsizes)?

There remains the question of uncertainty with regard to the date, and we must recognize that this is a very uncomfortable situation.

Certainly, when we are still young, when our health is good, when our country is not in a state of war, the question hardly poses itself. We make long-term commitments, and we do not ask ourselves whether "we will have time." But when we perceive that our duration is soon to end, everything gets complicated. Uncertainty is hard to bear. But is it any easier to bear the certainty?

What can be the real interior state of a condemned man who knows beforehand the day of his execution? I think also of the man who, for serious reasons, urged his doctor to tell him how much time he had left, because he knew that he had cancer of the liver; the doctor told him that he could undoubtedly count on two or three months. Was it right to do so, or was it wrong? The next day, the sick man committed suicide.

Is it better to know or not to know when we will die? I think that it is impossible to answer this question. But isn't it simpler to take things as they come—that is, to really embark on the voyage of duration, in the certainty-uncertainty which, deep down, is essentially stimulating, especially if we perceive its dynamic and "preparatory" character?

CHAPTER THREE

With Regard to Suicide

According to an old legend, tenacious like all errors, the scorpion, when it is surrounded by a circle of burning embers and it "sees that it is lost," inserts its stinger between its armor. This is false. The scorpion simply ends up by being grilled in the zig-zags it makes to escape.

Suicide is a specifically human fact. It is bound up with consciousness of agony, even if the latter is inscribed in the most obscure subconsciousness. I think that without extrapolating we can say that it is bound up with a certain apprehension of the dialectic of duration, such as we have discussed it.

The *idea* of suicide is common. I mean by this that we cannot be ignorant of its possibility and that everyone, at some time or other, talks about it, undoubtedly with regard to a striking item in the news or to a drama among one's circle of relatives. But to speak about something, we have to have an idea of it. And since it is a matter of death, we cannot not be directly concerned by the idea that we can provoke it ourselves.

Undoubtedly, few persons can really affirm that the idea of suicide has *never* brushed close to them, even if it passed quickly and was immediately exorcised. It is perhaps those who protest the loudest ("Never once have I ever thought of committing suicide!") who have *unconsciously* been the most tempted to do so. And, usually, those who do commit suicide are persons who spoke of it to no one beforehand.

But whereas the *idea* of suicide is almost universal, the *fact* of suicide is really quite rare if we consider its statistical proportion. We can get the impression that it occurs frequently, but this conclusion is reached in much the same way as the one we reach after reading the Monday newspapers with regard to the auto accidents which happened over the weekend. Their number seems enormous until we compare it to the total number of people who were out driving at that time.

Moreover, we can say that suicide is always pathological conduct, despite any appearances of problems of "nervous equilibrium" or "mental health." I do not think that this affirmation is made only to reassure us—that is, to situate us outside of the pathological. There is, in fact, a "collapse," a "depressive crisis," which can take place without the least sign of warning, or be preceded by certain indices whose significance can be grasped by the informed observer *only afterward.* A break in the will to live is usually felt to be *abnormal,* although it is explainable in some dramatic instances. And we can spend a long time discussing whether suicide is an act of cowardice or of courage! The problem is not of this order.

In fact, in relation to death, we react in a way that we can compare to what we feel in the presence of a void. Some people "do not feel vertigo"—that is, they confront the void with a kind of security in being careful not to fall into it. Others "feel vertigo"—that is, they feel the paradoxical and positive attraction of the void.

I think we can say that there really is a "vertigo in the face of death," and that few people escape it, one day or another, although most conquer it.

This break introduced by someone in the apprehension of his own duration is very strange. What can its meaning be?

We often hear of auto-aggressiveness. Since the subject can no longer situate his aggressiveness positively in the world that surrounds him, he turns it against himself—as in the legend of the scorpion. We should notice that it is the people who do not commit suicide who say this. And if such a formula corresponds to a superficial and simplistic approach to things, it does not account for what happens in reality. It seems to me much more accurate to say that suicide is first of all a *language*. It is a way for the subject "to express something to someone."

In this sense, no true suicide attempt, however it may have miscarried, is ever to be regarded lightly. There is a great difference between a simulated suicide and a suicide which fails. The person who takes two sleeping pills in order to sleep well, leaving four empty bottles on his night-table to make it appear that he has swallowed that many pills, has taken no risk; he is really playing a game. However, the person who swallows four bottles of pills, but whose plight is discovered before it is too late, really risks his life. This is no longer comedy; he is not *playing,* and his language becomes a genuinely real call, although a spectacular one.

In any case, suicide is designed to affect other persons, as is also true of simulation on quite another level. The ancient philosopher who threw himself into the crater of Mount Etna took the precaution of leaving his sandals on the edge. And if he had not left them, the absence of any indication, along with his disappearance, would have made people talk about him still more. When we affirm something or pose a question, we are always addressing someone else.

This introduces us to an inextricable complexity, because each case is strictly singular, as much as any other form of "conversation," and no "general law" can be extracted. The most we can do is give a few examples of this "intentionality" of suicide, whether it be conscious or not.

First of all, to whom is the suicide addressed? The first idea that comes to mind is that it is addressed to the people who surround the person in everyday life. But it is not as simple as this. Psychoanalysis shows us to what point our actual relations are suspended from our primitive affective experiences. There is the process of overdetermination whose result is that an old conflictual situation which was not resolved can somehow be reproduced, relived and intensified in an actual situation. Let us take the example—perhaps not so theoretical as our description may lead us to believe—of a man who commits suicide; he married a woman of the same type who reproduces to a degree the conflictual relationship. His suicide, whose signification is necessarily very ambivalent, is undoubtedly addressed as much to his mother as to his wife.

When a subject commits suicide during the time he is undergoing psychoanalysis, his act is also addressed to the psychoanalyst. Thus we can understand why a competent practician thinks twice before beginning a long-term treatment, because it is undoubtedly quite a burden to bear.

But what does the person mean who addresses his suicide to an "other" person in such a consistent and imprecise way? The meanings are very diverse. Everything happens as if he wants, by means of the irreparable, to put the other person in a situation of fundamental *uneasiness*. Contrary to appearances, the suicide is perhaps still more aggressive against the "other" person than against himself. He seeks to punish the other person, to make him feel guilty, to make him feel agony, to frustrate him irremediably.

But this causes us to pose a singular problem. How can the idea of suicide occur if it does not imply the possibility of "enjoying the spectacle"? How can a person commit suicide if he does not have *beforehand* the idea that he will be able to "see" what happens? Once again, we are confronted by the insoluble dialectic between consciousness and duration.

I recall the case of a 15-year-old boy who, in the midst of a crisis of depression, set out one morning to get himself run over by a train. At the last minute, he merely put his foot over the rail, and he had to have a leg amputated. Actually— and he was conscious of the fact—he wanted, as he himself said, "to be crippled in order to get even," but he wanted so much to be sure of *seeing* it that he committed only what we might call partial suicide. The psychoanalytical view of a case of this type contains very complex data and very rich significance.

Thus the suicide may desire to trouble another person's complacency. But when it is a matter of death, can't this language, which is addressed to the "other" person, go so far as to be addressed to God, whatever the psychological or metaphysical content of this word may be? I know of cases of suicide which, as paradoxical as this may seem, were acts of faith.

Another signification of suicide, one that is evident at first sight, consists in what we can call flight from the intolerable. It is not unrelated to the preceding one, because the intolerable is always lived in one way or another in relation to others.

The old man who hangs himself because he is alone addresses himself to others inasmuch as they are absent—whether dead or indifferent. The ruined financier who shoots himself in the head flees the intolerable situation of "losing his honor" in the eyes of other people.[1] The member of the underground resistance who swallows cyanide, fearing that he will be forced to talk through intolerable torture, acts to save his companions and to increase the culpability of his executioners.

I recall the case of a 19-year-old boy who attempted suicide three times, of which the last, with barbiturates, almost succeeded. This boy apparently had no reason to kill himself. Had he wanted to, with proper help, he could have found a meaning to his existence. But under his smiling and timid exterior, an unsuspected despair gnawed at him. His mother had never told him who his father was, and she refused to do so—she was herself seriously neurotic. His impossibility to

---

[1] It would be interesting to study what this notion of "honor" really contains or represents. The way in which the other person sees the subject is quite evidently predominant, but what is its role, and isn't its importance deceiving on the level of human values? I have always found it absurd and revolting that a ship's captain, once he has assured himself that everyone is saved, should go down with his ship "for honor's sake." There are some acts of suicide, if we may say so, that have no "justification."

situate himself in reference to a man was really intolerable for him; he found many adults who acted as "fathers" to him, but what he needed was to know who *his own* was. His suicide was simultaneously a flight, since life had no meaning for him, and a dramatic cry to his mother, who did not understand it.

In some circumstances, however, flight from the intolerable is more dominant than the other signification. For example, the person with incurable cancer who kills himself in order not to suffer is not speaking to an "other" person in the way we have described it up to now. But we can ask whether the language is addressed, then, to the "other" called God. Vague interlocutor or not, concept or mystery, he is always "a live circuit," at least implicitly. To deny someone is the ultimate way of positing his existence. And to say that he does not exist is to provoke him to manifest himself.

But what does "flight from the intolerable" mean? We must first of all note that many people surmount the "intolerable," often for a long time, without committing suicide. It is sufficient merely to mention all of the cases of incurable cancer and all of the abandoned old people who do not commit suicide. Some personalities are subject to vertigo. But we will return to this question later.

It is always a matter, necessarily, of something *actually* intolerable for which no possible solution can be foreseen. The man who commits suicide does not suppress his desire, which is the very foundation of his existence as a subject, but he wants to get out of a situation which, precisely, contradicts his desire too much. Once again we return to the dialectic between the subject and his duration. Actually, he does not desire *to no longer be*—since this is inconceivable, as we have seen—but "to live no longer under these conditions." Popular language expresses this well when it comments: "He has left for a better world." And this reflection, quite instinctive, is well made, in passing, to reassure those who caused the intolerable situation without, *for the moment,* truly experiencing it.

I do not think it is paradoxical to say that, psychologically speaking, the subject who commits suicide has nothing but this negative way to affirm that he exists. He feels that his life is so denied, or misunderstood, on levels and for reasons which are infinitely diverse, that he can no longer affirm his "I" except by showing by means of his suicide how much he is still master of it. At the limit, he shows that he *can* kill *himself* —in other words, that he exists *to that point*.

And there is always an "afterward" in the perspective of suicide. This "afterward" cannot be conceived of as duration, if we really reflect on it, except in a mythical concept, but it can be conceived of only as being. The word "afterward" has itself no apprehensible sense, no more than does the expression "on the other side," which is of the spatial order. But it remains nonetheless true that the subject cannot conceive of himself, other than as consciousness of himself when he thinks about killing *himself*, as being in "another mode." Even unknown to the subject and contrary to what he may think or write before his act, suicide is undoubtedly, in the very pathology which it represents, a paroxysmal affirmation of being. Certainly, we can explore no more than this side of the event, but it is quite striking.

We often fail to ask even elementary questions because they are unusual ones—or, more exactly, because they are embarrassing and open up disagreeable or worrisome perspectives.

And yet, there is one that is not without interest. Why, when we see someone who is going to commit suicide, do we instinctively feel a desire to stop him? This question is posed here on the level of psychological investigation.

With rare exceptions, it is a common reaction. It has even inspired legislation. If a person in despair throws himself into the Seine, while a spectator looking on does nothing to prevent him, the latter can be prosecuted for "not assisting a person in danger," provided that someone witnessed his attitude. And if he answers that he did not feel he had a right to interfere with someone else's freedom—in this case, of the man in despair—

I think that his answer would be very poorly understood and would cause scandal. And yet this attitude of neutrality could very well be neither indifference nor cowardice, but a truly great respect for the mystery of the other person, although it be poorly understood.

What is there, then, in this spontaneous and almost universal reaction which tends to prevent someone from committing suicide? This is undoubtedly not a simple question.

In the somewhat particular situation where someone lets you know that he is really thinking about committing suicide, it is a bit easier to understand it. James comes to me, tells me of his problems, and says quite clearly that he is going to kill himself. The reason is to signify something to me; otherwise, he would not have come to speak to me and to ask something of me. My first reflex is that he is asking me "to help him not to do it," and if I were not to stop him by means of my arguments or action from really committing suicide, I would not be answering what he is asking of me. But there is no proof at all that such is the real meaning of his coming to me. He is perhaps coming merely to ask of me that I recognize his idea of suicide as explainable or, in a sense, "legitimate." Perhaps he only wishes me to show him that I understand, and that *in his situation* the same idea would also come to me. This attitude permits him the necessary "distance" to be able to confront or command the situation. At most, feeling both my understanding and the respect which I am trying to have for his suffering, not feeling himself judged as a monster and not finding himself vehemently called "back to reason," he will not be given an additional burden of supplementary guilt and will be able to come out of it more easily. But to achieve this, I must reach the point where I do not *desire for personal reasons* that he give up his idea of suicide. If someone comes to speak to me in this way, it is because, in general, he wants me to "help him to live." But I am neither he, nor God. Am I going to complicate the situation by letting my own fear or my eagerness to be in good conscience interfere? I must first of all help him to live.

The 19-year-old boy who tried to commit suicide three times successively began to approach his problems of existence more positively when he understood that I would truly exercise no constraint and that it would not disturb me seriously if he should attempt it again. Besides, when someone goes around saying that he is going to commit suicide, we can generally assume that he is not going to do it simply because he has said it.

The more difficult situation is the one in which we have a presentiment that someone is "in danger of" committing suicide, but without his mentioning it clearly. We feel concerned in quite another way. In this case, I do not think that a dominant part is played by fear of eventual guilt that we may have for not having "taken charge" of someone else's existence and therefore, in a sense, having killed him. It is more complex and more profound. Not situated as a "possible savior," we are confronted more crudely with our own certitude of frailty.

When the subject who I think is contemplating suicide asks *nothing* of me whenever I see him or when I talk with him, in a sense this is worse. In the first place, I am "cut off," not recognized as able to give anything (and this is really very frustrating). Moreover, by that very fact, it is not so much the other person's personal problem that confronts me, as it is my own vertigo in the face of death, my own "certainty-uncertainty," my own fundamental *question,* without any possible protection or alibi. (I was going to say: with the underlying reasons which I, myself, might have for thinking of suicide.)

And in this, it is not so much with my death as such that I am confronted, but with the real agony of the freedom I have to provoke it. When I see someone die as the result of an accident or some incurable sickness, this evokes for me the caducity which I *undergo* of my own duration, and that thought is difficult enough to bear. But when I see someone who attempts suicide—whether he fails or not—I really feel vertigo; it is no longer a matter of a destiny which I must undergo, but more of an event which I, *myself*, can provoke. There are times when a person's idea of his own power— evoked by what he sees—can literally make him afraid, because it corresponds, in a way, to a *desire:* the desire to affirm oneself, the paradoxical desire to be beyond time, the desire for liberation. On certain levels or at certain times, isn't the desire to live very near to the "desire to die"? All of the fundamental ambivalence of human reality lived is exposed violently to daylight by someone who commits suicide—this ambivalence whose depth has been revealed by psychoanalysis. We will return to this later.

I remember an authentic story, a somewhat banal one, which situates suicide in very complex perspectives. A man came to the sacrament of confession. He said that he had just swallowed a large quantity of barbiturates and that he was going to return home to die, but he wanted first of all to receive absolution for the serious sin of having shortened his days—a very complex attitude: fear and avowal of guilt, but with the idea that the priest, bound by the secret of confession, could say nothing.

By a very rare coincidence, the priest in question was also a doctor, formerly connected with hospital work, who had retained what might be called a "basic medical reflex." Without waiting, he leaped out of the confessional, grabbed the penitent by the collar, dragged him out, turned him around and quickly convinced him to let himself be taken to the nearest hospital. An ambulance was summoned, and there followed emergency hospitalization, stomach pumping and a proper dose of strychnine. Fifteen days later, the man came to thank the priest for having saved him.

I leave the reader the freedom to think what he wants of this. But it is interesting to ask the true meaning of the "client's" demand, as well as that of the confessor's reaction. The least we can say is that both were in immediate contact with death, as a personal event, and that the confessor, besides, was concerned by his anterior professional commitment.

There is another incongruous question with regard to suicide, which can clarify the problem of the unexpected day.

The first thing that comes to mind, naturally, is the question of why people commit suicide. Statistics can be established (with the very debatable significance of all statistics): despair, misery, deception in love, etc. It can go so far as the act of a man who, threatened with death for one reason or another, kills himself "in order not to have to look forward to death anymore"—like Gribouille who submerged himself in water when it rained.

But there is, nevertheless, one very important piece of evidence. Nearly everyone, at some time or other, is subject to despair. As little as we open our eyes to it, misery is outrageously frequent, revolting and often sordid. The deceptions of love, perhaps more cruel than anything else, are very common. And yet suicide is rare. There is no common measure between the frequency of suffering which we estimate as intolerable and the frequency of suicide.

Certainly, the suffering of the other person is always inappreciable. In other words, when I see a human being in a situation—*which is not mine*—which I would not bear, I can in no way understand interiorly how he lives it, bears it and resolves it. I can say to myself that "if such a thing were to happen to me, I could not survive it," and then perceive sometime later that the "thing" has happened to me and that I am surviving it without hardly thinking about it. Besides, it is striking to note that suicide is clearly more frequent in countries where—apparently—misery has best been conquered.

Then comes the incongruous question: *"Why don't people commit suicide?"* If we follow the human drama closely enough without closing our eyes, we would see that suicide should logically be more frequent. But it is not.

If our profession brings us to receive men and women whose difficulties of existence are apparently without solution, there comes a time when we ask ourselves why it is that one or another has not committed suicide or does not think about suicide. This would tempt us to think that the impulse to suicide—or the "pre-disposition" to it—is inscribed as a pathological tendency in the very primitive affective structures. It is essential for the child to have acquired a minimum of certitude regarding himself as seen by other people if he is not to be in danger, later, of looking upon his own death as the only solution possible in extreme situations.

But this having been said, the question remains: Why do so many people who are in apparently intolerable difficulty not even think of doing away with themselves? Certainly, it can be because of a conscious and positive concern for the persons around them, not wishing to plunge them into embarrassment, confusion or catastrophe. But there is undoubtedly also a much deeper factor. We can situate it in the unreasoned and predominant impression that "it is not finished," that "tomorrow something will happen," that "tomorrow I will find a way." In other words, the dialectic between the "I" and duration then acts in a positive and stimulating way.

This implies, first of all, not only that "I" feel myself really existing, but also that tomorrow is possible with all its *unforeseen* events. It is necessary that I feel this tomorrow as a margin of incertitude where my aggressiveness will find its insertion and exercise possible, and that there remain in me, in a sense, not only a *taste* for fighting, but also a "place" to do it.

It is easy to conceive that in a civilization where everything is almost completely foreseen and organized, where the possibility of "riot" is reduced to a minimum, where social organization assures each one of finding a future legislated beforehand, suicide would become a real epidemic, especially among young people. Such a civilization would constitute a world of *tedium* where, according to G. Hahn's expression, people would have all the *means* for living, but from that very fact have no more *reason* to do so. According to convergent testimonies, certain Nordic civilizations conform somewhat to this picture. It is in constructive confrontation with a world which is impermeable beforehand that the personality becomes conscious of itself. On its level, psychoanalysis demonstrates this in what pertains to the affective evolution of the child.

Sometimes people say to me that their life has no more meaning for them and that they ask themselves "why they are alive." It is somewhat as though they were asking me to tell them (which, in the perspective of the psychology of the subconscious, is charged with the significance of a demand that is obscure and complex in a different way than it seems to be at first).

In fact, it is a very embarrassing situation. What should one answer? If we exclude the formula learned in the catechism, which does not make much existential sense—"we are placed on earth to know God, to love him and to serve him"— we are really caught short. And we are confronted with this question for ourselves, a question which we usually omit asking: "Indeed, why am I living?" *Why?* All of the answers we can give are really deceiving or insufficient. The only one which has some consistency is: "I am living in order to be me right to the end, and suicide interrupts something. That's enough of a reason." (And this answer undoubtedly conforms to the idea of creation contained in Judaeo-Christian revelation: God calling me to be myself as much as possible in my relations of love with other "me's" as my response to him.)

I do not think it is a gratuitous extrapolation to say that, normally, we feel a kind of transcendence of life, as if it were in itself dependent on "something other" than ourselves. And this is also one of the reasons for which, normally, we do not commit suicide. Indeed, we often note that those people who do not know why they live continue to do so and do nothing to prevent it.

What of the fear of the unknown? Basically such fear somewhat resembles the man who is sick of living in the suburbs, but who does not come to the city because he is "not sure what it will be like."

What of the fear of unleashing the anger or reprisals of Someone? Essentially, killing oneself is an act of independence as dangerous as it is for the adolescent to stand up to the authority of his father. Whether we are explicitly "believers" or whether we loudly affirm our unbelief, it seems to me that reference is always made to this Someone more or less precise, more or less named, a "Someone" whose demand would be criminally misunderstood if we killed ourselves. We have "to wait until he decides that we should die." Then, in a sense, death takes on the meaning of response to a plan, whereas suicide would be its refusal. This may be poorly stated, but it is very difficult to express adequately. This "Someone" corresponds first of all to a projection, an undebatable one, of the parental image, developed by cultural environment. This projection should not be confused with the "idea of God" given by Judaeo-Christian revelation. If we do not disfigure it—as it is easy to do and frequently done—the latter is a much more profound concept, with a far different approach to the meaning of death, even though the first psychological apprehension of it is conditioned by the common elements to which we are referring.

In summary, there is a dialectical tension which comes into play at moments of despair: the desire for deliverance, and fear of the unknown and of the "Other." Usually, this second instance is the stronger and brings the subject to the level of what we can call hope—that is, the impression that the desired deliverance will take place *in duration*. The truly Christian perspective is vaster, but we will treat of it only at the end of this book.

What remains is the fact that suicide is rare. It seems that the structure of "wanting to live at any price" is the more normal one. That structure collapses into suicide when diverse factors have been present during the evolution of childhood, factors which have not permitted sufficient solidity of the affective personality to be established. But this is only a very imperfect way of expressing our thought.

This reference to the "Other"—whatever we call it, even if it is only to refute it—is undebatable, at least implicitly. For men on a dramatic road, might this not be the very first stage of what could one day be faith in this Other, finally known as he has *revealed himself?*

CHAPTER FOUR

Death and Science

According to the laws of all civilized countries, a doctor has the responsibility of certifying death—that is, of deciding beyond any further discussion that a person is dead. It is the medical profession which defines death. But what is death, medically speaking?

This is, in fact, a very embarrassing question, because it is necessary to admit that nothing is known about it. The only answer that can be given is a truism: "It is when someone ceases to live." Medicine does not know what death is; it can only decipher its signs and apparent causes, but the profound reality of death escapes it. The pathological or "natural" mechanisms (aging) which result in the fact of death are more or less explained, but knowledge goes no farther. The most important thing in practice is recognition of the signs which enable the fact to be affirmed, and this for concrete reasons such as burial, the administration of a will, civil status, etc.

But regarding this precise question concerning the positive signs of death, we have to admit that at this moment in history we are no further advanced in our ability to determine the precise moment of death than we were in the far distant past. When we think of the tremendous progress that has been made in our scientific knowledge of fertility, the development of life, the signs of the beginning of the existence of a human being before his birth, it is rather disconcerting to realize that we are still in complete ignorance or reduced to vain mutterings in regard to the signs of death.

The two criteria of death——clinical and official——are simple: the cessation of breathing and of circulation—the sign of a mirror placed in front of the mouth, and auscultation of the heart. Some worried people, fearing the insufficiency of these signs and a tardy awakening in their casket, request that at their death an artery be cut to be sure that the blood is no longer circulating.

But we have to admit that these signs are very crude. The death of someone is not so simple, because, physiologically, it takes place over a rather long period of time. At most, and paradoxically, we can say that we are never *sure* of someone's death until we begin to observe undeniable signs of decomposition.

Hair, beard and fingernails continue to grow for at least twenty-fours hours after the mortuary grooming has been completed. It is not unusual for a particularly hairy deceased person, for aesthetical reasons, to have to be shaved several hours "afterward," so that he will be "presentable" during the wake. On the other hand, some organs change and begin to decompose very quickly, like the suprarenals, but a particularly delicate surgical operation would be necessary to observe them.

What have changed very much are the relatively recent and spectacular advances made in reanimation. They have made very evident the radical insufficiency of the classical signs of death in certain cases. By means of complicated techniques of transfusion and artificial respiration, we can, for example, maintain life in wounded persons who are apparently dead—that is, whose heartbeat and respiration would stop if nothing were done. For some, it happens that spontaneous life is resumed and they are "resurrected," as the newspapers say. For others, the artificial maneuvers can last for months, but as soon as they are stopped, everything stops. To a mind formed in a scientific spirit and which does not let itself be influenced by the commercial romanticism of the press, this simply means that the latter were really dead and that the former were not. In both cases, the classical signs of death were deceiving; the stopping of the heart and of circulation did not signify the death of the first as subjects; the artificial cardiac and pulmonary functioning in the second masked the fact that they were dead as subjects.

It is therefore necessary to find another criterion, a surer one, especially since a practical problem is now being posed, and we have reason to believe that it will become more serious: the transplanting of organs. Technically, vital organs can be taken from persons under artificial animation to be grafted onto persons whom they might be able to save. But we find ourselves facing a scruple: if the person in coma who is under reanimation is living, we run the danger of killing him. This amounts to saying, in other words, that at the present time we can maintain the vegetative life of a body while the person is dead; the problem is to be sure that he is. These technical advances—developed especially since World War II —inspired Jean Rostand, in an interview, to state one of those touching and romantically naive statements of which it is good to beware: "I have often said and written that a dead person is someone temporarily incurable." Taken literally, this "magnificent" sentence runs the danger of rushing us into the world of "science fiction."

In May 1966, the Academy of Medicine gave a new definition to the certain signs of death. According to the Academy, in doubtful cases death is to be determined clinically by the "death of the brain"; this judgment is to be made by means of an electro-encephalogram. If it is rectilinear—that is, manifesting the disappearance of all electric current—at the end of forty-eight hours, we can affirm, in the actual state of science, that the *subject* is dead, even if vegetative life persists, maintained by the artifice of reanimation.

We should not conclude from this that modern medicine is trying to "master" death. It is only situating it more exactly as the "global" and personal event of an individual. In other words, it can only give a greater degree of certitude regarding the fact of death, but it is rather striking to note that this criterion, although founded scientifically in a particularly serious manner, remains essentially a "convention."

Medicine's relation to death has greatly changed in history at the same time as the medical attitude itself has changed in relation to the phenomenon of sickness. In *Naissance de la Clinique* (The Birth of Clinical Science),[1] Michel Foucault has made a remarkable study of this change, which is, after all, only a particularly striking aspect of the cultural change introduced in human thought by the appearance of the scientific *attitude* through the development of the sciences, especially since the 17th century.

One of the most important stages of development in regard to our topic was the appearance of clinical anatomy—that is, research on a cadaver to find the causes of its death and the "mechanism" of the sickness which provoked it. This attitude of research by autopsy is a self-evident reflex for modern medicine, to such a degree that it is hard to believe that its appearance is so recent. Actually, it dates from the beginning of the last century, dominated by the name of Bichat, and constitutes a real revolution in thought. Michel Foucault expresses it vividly:

"In 18th-century medical thought, death was simultaneously an absolute fact and the most relative of phenomena. It was the end of life, and likewise that of sickness if its nature was fatal; at death, the sickness reached the end of its course, became silent, and was reduced to a memory. But if it happened that traces of the sickness ate into the cadaver, then no evidence could determine what resulted from the sickness and what resulted from death; their signs criss-crossed in undecipherable disorder—so much so that death was an absolute, from the point of which there was no longer either life or sickness, but its disorganizations were the same as all morbid phenomena. Clinical experimentation, in its first form, did not question this ambiguous concept of death" (p. 142).

". . . Life, sickness and death now constitute a technical

[1] Presses universitaires de France, 1963.

and conceptual trinity. The old continuity of centuries-old obsessions which saw in life the threat of sickness, and in sickness the approaching presence of death, is broken; in its place, there is set up a triangular figure whose summit is defined by death. It is from the height of death that we can see and analyze the organic dependencies and pathological sequences. Instead of being what it was for so long, this night in which life is erased, and in which sickness itself is confused, is gifted forevermore with the great power of enlightenment which dominates and brings to light both the space of the organism and the time of the sickness. . . . Its privilege of intemporality, which is undoubtedly as old as consciousness of its imminence, has been made for the first time a technical instrument which enables us to grasp the truth of life and the nature of its ailment. Death is the great analyst which shows connections by unraveling them and manifests the wonders of genesis in the rigor of decomposition—and the word *decomposition* must be left to stumble in the heaviness of its meaning. An analysis of the elements and of their laws finds in death what it had searched for in vain in mathematics, chemistry and even in language: an unsurpassable model, one prescribed by nature; and medical vision will base itself henceforth on this great example. It is no longer the vision of a living eye, but that of one which has seen death—a great white eye that unravels life" (p. 145-146).

". . . It was undoubtedly a very difficult and paradoxical task for medical vision to work such a conversion. An immemorial inclination, as old as the fear of men, had turned the eyes of doctors toward the elimination of sickness, toward healing, toward life; it could only be a matter of restoring it. Death remained to the doctor the great somber menace which neutralized his knowledge and his skill; it was a danger not only to life and sickness, but also to the knowledge which questioned them. With Bichat, medical vision pivoted on itself and asked death to account for life and sickness, and its definitive immobility to account for their time and movements. Didn't medicine have to invert its oldest anxiety in order to read, in what manifested its failure, what should be the foundation of its truth?" (p. 148).

Indeed, this represents a real reversal in thought, and certainly not only from the scientific viewpoint. We can say that from then on, man considered his death in quite another way. It was integrated both as an element of his history and as the object of scientific study. Until modern times, death was merely *undergone;* now, it is *studied.* We can see in this change of attitude a kind of attempt at domination. But this domination tends more to suppress death than to look for its meaning. It is no longer considered as an exterior element, as an "accident," but it is accepted as "inscribed in the nature of things" and as partially accessible to knowledge.[2] For this, it was necessary to overcome a kind of "fright," one which, however, is inscribed in the general development of the scientific attitude. "Magical fear" of the "forces of nature" has been conquered by the need to know.

In what concerns death, as medically studied since the last century, the consequences of this change in attitude are very complex. Although we have been able to acquire this "mastery" which enables us to approach and to use death to understand life and sickness better, the question concerning death itself has nevertheless not been resolved. Instead, we are confronted by its massive certitude more cruelly than ever, and by continued confirmation of the impossibility of any escape. We know that death *is,* and that it is one of the fundamental laws of life. Under its various forms, benign or serious, sickness generally is, in a way, only its more or less remote preamble.

If we conceive of medicine, in the human effort, as the

[2] This implies a necessary change in the way of speaking of death in other disciplines. If we can no longer speak of an "accident," we can no longer consider that death did not *always take place.* Neither can we consider it as a "punishment for an act of foolishness," which would mean that it was contingent. This brings us to take better account of the meaning of the first chapters of Genesis. They are not a scientific or historical document in the modern sense of the term; their meaning, expressed symbolically, is much more profound, true and mysterious than was ever imagined.

battle against death *in order to suppress it,* it is difficult to appreciate the claims which modern medicine makes of this continually recurring illusion. This is particularly true in view of the contradiction that, having at its disposition ever more efficacious helps to overcome sicknesses, medicine realizes its abject powerlessness to basically resolve the human drama—that is, sickness and death. It "postpones" the event, from the viewpoint of general statistics, but it makes its character of inevitability all the more conspicuous. In paradoxical terms, we can say that nothing exists that is as "abnormal" as sickness and death, and that modern medicine, with its impressive arsenal of knowledge and possibilities, ends up by showing us that, in the last analysis, the most "normal" thing there is is to end by dying. In a sense, death has become "familiar," but its opacity remains complete and is affirmed as radically impenetrable.

Therefore, we can understand why, in a rational and scientific world like ours, real "upsurges of horror" take place, sometimes of surprising irrationality or childishness. In regard to cancer, automobile accidents and other means of destruction, we meet the same reflex action: we battle against death with the underlying illusion that we will "reach a solution."

I think that the phenomenon of healers is a significant expression of this upsurge of horror. Certainly, and quite evidently, there have always been men and women "gifted with powers" to heal or to right what is wrong. But it is striking that a revival of these phenomena—bound up with all kinds of "mystical" beliefs, from Christian Science to more or less doubtful "apparitions" or "miracles"—should occur just at the time when medicine has finally become scientific. It is undoubtedly related to the fact that so-called official medicine remained exclusively organic up to present times, and did not integrate the specifically human dimension which psychology has introduced since the time of Freud.[3] But I think that it is also due to the fact that death, having become a subject of

---

[3] Cf., by the same author, *Médecins et Guérisseurs* (Doctors and Healers), Lethielleux, 1955.

interest to science, imposes itself as a reality of life as fundamental and as irreversible as birth. In a sense, death has lost its poetic or philosophical fascination and become an existential question, one without an answer, and we can no longer not perceive it in its prosaic brutality.

Therefore, we flee from it. And it is quite remarkable that recourse to the "occult" of medicine—from the most obviously puerile to the most pretentiously pseudo-scientific—is no longer reserved primarily to the less-educated strata of the population. We are surprised to see the number of technicians and graduates holding high degrees in very "evolved" subjects who unhesitatingly have recourse to the "occult" as soon as their health is at stake. This is because official modern medicine merely *treats* an illness, and does not guarantee against death, whereas the "healer," we might say, heals blindly and maintains the illusion of "indefinite duration," which science can no longer admit.

This reminds me of a dialogue which took place after a public lecture on healers. A man in the audience, with great emotion—I should say, with agony, although I did not realize it at the time—rose and asked me: "But, sir, when medicine cannot really do anything more for a sick person, his only recourse is the healer!" And I answered, "Good heavens, no, sir; there is still the anointing of the sick."

Under this debatable form of wit, I meant to say precisely what he could not bear; modern medicine treats and prolongs life in a way that is rather spectacular, but at the same time, at least implicitly, it admits that despite all of its arsenal it cannot change the human condition, which is *mortality*.

As strange as it may seem, even some doctors cannot face this evidence, and this leads to naive beliefs that are almost as puerile as those of the healers. I heard one university professor declare publicly, without the least realization of the ridiculous, that modern medicine has reached the point where it can strangle every illness. I felt like telling him—but it would not have "registered"—that, excluding a few illnesses for which we cannot do much, there is at least one for which we can do nothing: it completes the cycle, whatever it be, and its symptom—a universal one—can be called "shortness of breath." As popular language says, "Everyone dies of something." And this sums up the whole problem of medicine.

Is death a failure on the part of medicine? This is the basic question, which amounts to asking what, after all, is the sense of this discipline, both scientific and creative, that is said to be at the service of "health" and "life."

Unavoidably, I am urged to reflect here on two personal memories. While I was working a long time ago as a replacement surgeon in a small city, I was called to the hospital one night for an emergency case. The ambulance had just brought in a poor woman, a Spaniard who spoke very little French. She had tried to commit suicide. The situation was a rather strange one: she had a large abdominal tumor, and she had been told that an operation was necessary, but she despaired of putting her domestic affairs in order, and she had not managed to bring herself to enter surgery. And so, she took a pair of scissors (which she had heated!), and she opened a rather large umbilical hernia, making an incision into the peritoneum, after which she slit her wrists in a rather superficial way. Hardly half an hour had passed since she had done this; the peritoneum was open; she was in the operating room. Helped by an intern, I performed the operation which she had been so hesitant to undergo, and I took a huge cyst from her ovary. The rest was normal. Some days later, I left the city. Fifteen days later, the intern informed me that this woman had suddenly thrown herself from a fifth-floor window, on the very day that she was supposed to leave the hospital. My "victory" over death was therefore an illusory one.

At about the same time, I performed an emergency operation one night on a woman who had been brought to the hospital for a strangled hernia. It was a simple operation, caught in time; the rest was as normal, and she left the hospital fifteen days later. Had I not performed the operation, she would have been dead within forty-eight hours. But she had to die later—of something else. And since twenty years have passed since the time of the operation, I suppose it may be that she has been dead for some time. What, then, was the *power* of my surgical act? What sense, therefore, does medicine have in face of death?

I think this is a question of capital importance. In the light of science, the dialectic of power and weakness explodes. It is so intolerable that some medical attitudes become almost shocking. A certain reanimator, not able to bear the idea that his client was really dead, obstinately continued to attempt to restore life artificially, against all hope and even against the request of members of the family, who were no longer willing to allow the tragicomedy to continue on any level. His argument was that it was impossible to know. At least, the recent definition by the Academy of Medicine will settle any more such situations. If the electro-encephalogram continues to register nothing at the end of forty-eight hours, the *sick person* can be considered dead. It is probable that some doctors will not readily accept the fact that a new reference point—and a scientific one at that—has been placed on the limits of medical power.

What, therefore, is the *sense* of modern medicine? This is a question which I often asked myself while I was serving my internship. First of all, it "takes care of" people—in other words, it helps them to live. It tries to neutralize the "sickness" —that is, a difficulty of adaptation (a "disharmony") in someone with regard to his concrete existence, whether this "difficulty" is important or not, and whether its somatic side is or is not predominant in relation to its psychological side.

Medicine fights against sickness, and to do this, it tries to know it better scientifically. Moreover, since it concerns men and not animals, it extends from the most material biology to psychology which is most distinct from the "chemical" and the "physical," in an inseparable whole which modern science recognizes as such.

It fights against death, which sickness prefigures or prepares more or less remotely. But at present, it can no longer escape from the constraint of duration. In other words, it can only *postpone* death, and it has made spectacular progress in this regard, both in individual cases and on the statistical plane. But it *knows* that it can only *postpone* the collapse, this collapse being integrated, since the time of Bichat, as an object of study as universal as and more "observable" than life itself. This amounts to what the popular expression says: "Back up a bit to make a better jump." And what if medicine, basically, serves this end: to help men to take maximum advantage—in "quality" and in time—of their existence, in order to prepare better the capital event of their death?

The Doctor and Death

Undertakers and clergymen are always in close contact with death. I would say that they "use" it, and therefore that they are not entirely "against" it in their relation with it. It cannot appear to them as a failure. The former live on it, while the latter give it its meaning and, in principle, its reason for being.

What of the doctor? The choice of such a profession rarely occurs by accident. Usually, it rests on an attraction, an "inclination," a desire. The underlying motives can be very diverse, and are even inscribed in very primitive affective experiences. But in any case, they mark the subject as one who has consecrated himself to personal "combat" against "sickness and death."

When the doctor is faced with the latter—that is, when he sees one of his patients die despite his treatments—he is not only confronted with the general "failure" of duration; he is at the same time confronted with his personal failure concerning this failure. The echo, if we may call it this, is double.

Generally, the man who takes care of others considers himself as one who does not himself need to be cared for. (We could address to him a famous sentence from Scripture: "Doctor, cure yourself!") But this in no way prevents him from being, like everyone else, a dead man in potency. The death of one of his patients recalls this personal reality to him, as it does to everyone else. But it also denotes to him that, in the last analysis, there is nothing he can do against death, even though all of his life is oriented to "pushing it away."

The most surprising thing, after all, is that there are doctors, inasmuch as the great majority of them—implicitly or not—assume this fundamental contradiction. They accept the death of their patients without basic revolt—otherwise, they would quit the profession or commit suicide—and they recognize the limits of their powers. On reflection, for a question of such importance, this tends to prove that for them, even if they deny it, *death has sense*.

It is strange to ascertain that doctors are either "skeptics" or religious men, although often in traditional and inflexible forms. These are, after all, two ways of reacting to a very specific agony in this singular confrontation with death. Doctors are often reproached with being "individuals"; there is nothing surprising in this, because it results from a constant, particularly trying experience and one that is difficult to communicate. Scientific confrontations and exchanges are very possible, but the doctor's personal involvement in the face of life and death cannot be communicated, even indirectly, because it concerns too deeply what is embedded most firmly in the secret recesses of his inner self.

This can also explain, undoubtedly, a fact that is frequently observed: when a doctor, himself, acquires an incurable illness whose signs he knows very well, he is often subject to surprising blindness. The same signs in someone else would induce him to make a very quick diagnosis, but in himself, he avoids their meaning and rushes to reassuring explanations, which ordinarily he would dismiss with a smile. And, undoubtedly, it is not merely because he does not want to understand. The doctor's relation to his own death is more complex than that of other men.

This also underlies the attitude of "people," in general, toward doctors. It is known that this attitude is very ambivalent: we need them, but they make us afraid. But they are especially "crowned with a halo" by this complex relation with

their own death, this double "drama" of being mortals and of
being conquered: they are, among men, those who confront
the question in the name of the others, and who "lose their
skin" for it. Aren't they something like heroic volunteers who
attempt a desperate sortie?

The doctor-patient relationship is never an easy one,
especially collectively, because of this absolute certainty which
concerns both of them, but in such different ways.

Some years ago at Liège, a spectacular and far-reaching
incident became known. With the help of a doctor, a grand-
mother poisoned her daughter's baby, born without arms;
everyone around her had been convinced of the legitimacy
of this act. The doctor, still young and of the "generous" type,
had given out a prescription for the poison without having
personally seen the child.

The affective, social, and political implications in this
affair were very complex. But independently of this, it made
the doctors react, for it abruptly placed medical conscience
face to face with the fact of causing death, whatever be the
reason.

A doctor, by the specific choice of his profession is "at the
service of life," as they say, but at the same time he finds himself, by his scientific training and the technical means at his
disposal, in a special group of men who are in the best position
to kill without anyone knowing about it. Such is the temptation
of euthanasia.

At first sight, it is repugnant to the doctor to kill; there
would be something contradictory in it. But it is possible to
imagine an inverse attitude, a reaction, taking place. Faced
with an incurable case, a pathological fact which presents
itself as indicative of a total failure of all action possible to
him, the doctor who is completely committed to victory over
sickness and death can feel himself excessively concerned in
what we can call his narcissistic esteem. He is so deeply threatened in his own being that he is subject to the reflex idea of
"erasing" this proof of his powerlessness. It is not surprising

that this reaction can be observed—to varying degrees of control—in "idealistic" doctors—that is, in those whose deep, personal emotions there has not been integrated constructively the basic reality of failure as a factor of progress. Not without some fear, I one day heard a doctor declare vehemently that he felt it would be good to kill systematically all children born with serious abnormalities. We could feel in him a violent aggressiveness, hardly contained, which, without any doubt, was inscribed in the most tormented zones of his subconscious life.

But this reaction is rare. It seems that doctors, in general, go through the apprenticeship of failure progressively, perhaps without reflecting on it clearly. And in medical experience, it is a matter of the central and primordial failure, that of duration. The consciousness of the transitory nature of life, as a result of long intellectual discussions, is here a very strong factor. And usually it triumphs in the sense that the doctor, perhaps without even knowing it, reacts by witnessing to his personal observation that the "I" transcends duration. This corresponds to what we call, in moral language, respect for life and for person. I believe we can say that the doctor normally experiences this in a particularly realistic way and that it is not possible for him to treat the incurably sick person or child, as an intolerable object which must be destroyed.

Psychoanalysis and Death

One of the most important elements in the science of man is incontestably the world opened up by the discoveries of Freud. It is also, undoubtedly, the most disconcerting one, to the point that it still gives rise to resistance which can easily be qualified as passionate, if not desperate.

And it is not the least strange that, as he progressed in his study of affective dynamisms, Freud came to discover the existence of what he called "death instincts," in dialectical balance with "life instincts." The major text in this viewpoint is the one entitled, "Beyond the Principle of Pleasure" in

Essays in Psychoanalysis. According to very authoritative opinions, it seems that the French translation is unsatisfactory; the German word *triebe* does not correspond exactly to the French word for "instinct," but evokes a more complex dynamic reality in which the idea of "drive" and the idea of "force" play an important part. According to the specialists, we undoubtedly betray Freud's thought somewhat when we say simplistically that he spoke of a "death instinct." But the important thing is for the word to bring out the existence of an affective drive, not for the expansion of life, but, in a way, for its negation.

A few explanations are necessary here. It is not a matter of the expression of an aggressiveness, either toward another person or in a narcissistic return on oneself, which would seek to "destroy what lives." In "The Drives and Their Destiny," Freud shows that, in their evolution, the drives can undergo a real return to their contraries; love of self can change to hatred of self; love of the other can become "devouring."

But what Freud discovers "beyond the principle of pleasure" is a much more subtle reality. The affective drive which sets the child "on his way" in his conduct is the "principle of pleasure," confronted very quickly with the "principle of reality" which imposes on him a progressive structuration; but another drive appears, one just as strong, which we can properly call the "principle of repetition" or of "reproduction."

The child's conduct shows very well that he is led alternately by the search for satisfactory adaptation to new situations and by what Freud calls the "eternal return of the same." Perhaps it would be better to say "repetition which continues indefinitely." Tirelessly—for him, not for adults!—the child repeats a game which pleases him. As everyone knows, it is sometimes difficult to get him to stop without provoking tears or anger, the manifestations of intense frustration.

But this is equally observable in adult life, if only we watch for it. "Habits," after all, are nothing but a compromise between the two tendencies, and their ambiguity is not a recent discovery.

Friends spend a particularly enjoyable evening together; each feels deep satisfaction. Some days later, when they happen to meet again, they say, "It was marvelous! *If only we could relive it!*" They desire to duplicate exactly the evening already lived—in other words, literally to abolish everything that has happened since then, and to *relive* what they lived during those hours that, nevertheless, are in the past and beyond recall. Because, if we *relive* it eight days later, even if we try to reproduce the details and circumstances as faithfully as we can, it will not be the same and whether we want to admit it or not, it is quite possible that our reproduction will only be a painful caricature.

Therefore, in the deep source of affective life, there is a desire to "deny time," to abolish duration. But duration imposes itself as the very condition of life and this "desire for repetition" appears fatally as a "flight backward." One of the properties of life—and this is not its most accessible paradox —is that if we do not advance (principle of pleasure), we go backward. Thus, the principle of repetition cannot, in fact, reveal itself except as a "flight backward," a kind of counter-current, whose limit can be indicated: "premorulean non-being."[4] If I am driving a car and I pass another car which has stopped, the latter rapidly disappears behind me until it is no longer visible. This comparison can perhaps make it easier to understand the existential reality of this drive which is a "fixation on what is disappearing into the past"; and if we reflect on it, we see that it is a matter of a "death drive," because life is perpetual and progressive adoptive change.

This discovery by Freud, made on the level of clinical observation rendered possible by psychoanalysis, clearly manifests the basic dialectic of lived duration, the irremissible tendency to surpass time in time itself, or rather to "deny" it in a way, and to flow back toward the "non-living which was

[4] The "morula" is one of the first stages of the egg which began to be each one of us.

before the beginning." These reflections are not situated on a plane of philosophical, abstract and therefore serene meditation, but on the plane of apprehension of something lived which nothing can enable us to escape from now on; and we have to admit that this tends to make a person a little dizzy. It does not concern "man"; rather, it concerns *me,* and the other "me's" with whom I am in the complex and ambivalent relation of love or opposition.

It is striking to note that Freud, who discovered the "affective energies" in the progression and radiation of the conscious personality, did not believe in the illusion of a "superman" in time, in virtue of his discovery "beyond the principle of pleasure" of this strange constitutive drive which he calls—more or less incorrectly in his language or in the translation—the "death drive."

Biologically, as we have seen, the living structure of matter is specified by its tendency to perpetuate itself and by the caducity of individuals as such. This ambiguity, which is the death of the individual and his participation in maintaining the species, appears clearly on the level of sexual organization. Not being able to *reproduce* his very same self continually, he *reproduces* himself in the others who succeed him.

It is not surprising that the living human, who is knowledge and interrogative consciousness by his literally transcendent structure, lives this ambivalence in his affective ambivalence. The "death instinct" is therefore a kind of drive of the "me," in its battle against time which is precisely what makes it "die"—that is, suffer its death. The "life instincts," on the other hand, are logically connected to sexuality in the Freudian sense of the *sexuated* dynamic constitution of human reality.

All of this projects a completely new light onto the relations between love and death, a light much richer with unanswered questions than with reassuring intellectual statements.

Another aspect of this "principle of life"—"principle of repetition" dialectic appears on the level of the situation lived by the child from the time of his birth. We ascertain it, in fact, by observing reactions and conduct in light of what psychoanalysis enables us to understand and interpret.

Our existence begins with a profound "uneasiness." Immediately required to adapt to the exterior world for which, unlike an animal, he is in no way "prepared," the child manifests these two drives: the principle of pleasure and the principle of repetition. And in line with the latter, he shows what we can really understand to be—in terms that are evidently symbolical—a kind of nostalgia for his former state, a kind of "desire to return to the maternal womb." But, as obscure as it may be, the pre-consciousness of self which birth —the break by which the child *is*—established is irreversible. The very desire of "returning backward" gives rise to the threat of no longer *being distinct,* of being lived like a part of another person, of being in a way denied his subjective individuality, while still being "conscious" of this denial. If the break by which the child *is* tends to be completed, never able to be erased, agony arises. It is not an exaggeration to say that the human condition is this dialectic, established since the time of birth, between irreversible distinct existence and return to non-being, simultaneously "desired," in a way, and violently rejected in the instinctive battle against agony.

It is this instinctive battle which brings the child to find progressively his adaptive realizations in relation first with his mother and then with his father and with sexuated human contact, in the process properly designated by the term "sublimation." We now know that these first years are a continual succession of more or less intense conflicts in which, quite simply, survival as a subject is at stake. But the primitive agony, the dialectic between "I" and duration, is always latent and ready to rise up again at the least threat, even the most symbolic one. And it is according to his psychosomatic sex that the child situates himself in this battle which is never finished.

Such is the clinical conclusion which psychoanalysis has manifested: the strange and unexplainable "contradiction" between the individual subjective consciousness confronting its own duration in a fundamental uneasiness of progress and of immobilism and, on the other hand, this inability to move which tends to vertigo with the continual presentiment of non-being in an underlying manner, the ambivalent "threat" of death which, from the time of birth, can no longer be "lived" as annihilation, but as his *liberty* placed in question.

Once again, this conclusion is not of the philosophical order, but arises from attentive and methodical observation since the time of the Freudian discoveries; but this conclusion, nevertheless and quite evidently, gives rise to questions of another order. And I think that it is of value to emphasize that it poses them in an imperative way, not in the serene intemporality of intellectual speculations, but directly in the radical uncomfortableness of the lived.

CHAPTER FIVE

The Death of the Other Person

Death is nothing by itself; it is nothing but the end of something—or rather, of the existence of someone in the world. It is important to note that we can say no more about it; the only perception we have of death is that someone ceases to live—that is, to exist in a way that is verifiable and in time. In a sense, we are not exaggerating when we say that we cannot go beyond affirming that *someone's time "stops."*

This is as much as we can *know*. But, as Heidegger says, the very notion of stopping, of cessation, is fundamentally ambivalent. It can signify annihilation: when the old Trocadero was demolished, it ceased to exist. But it can also signify completion: when a painter has made his last brush stroke on a canvas, his work is finished; it *finally exists,* he hopes that it is indestructible, and he himself is "increased" by this work which is his. From the moment there is consciousness of self, *we can no longer eliminate* this second possible meaning.

As we have seen, I cannot experience my cessation, and I cannot even conceive of it or imagine it. The only experience I can have is the cessation of another person.

But the other person's death is not, strictly speaking, an experience of death, precisely because it is not to *me* that it is happening. It can be for me only an experience—an extremely complex and diverse one—of a radical change in my relationship to the other person, and therefore, to a degree and according to circumstances, a change in myself. In fact, we really *are* only in and by our multiple relations with other persons. And this essentially relational experience of self, which is existence, is absolutely incommunicable; although I can have some idea of the other person's relation to me, I can in no way have an idea of "the experience-as-lived-by-him." Sometimes the idea occurs to me that only his death enables the other person to know me just as I am, more perfectly than even I can know myself—in other words, that it is necessary for the other person to die for him to finally understand me.

The experience of another person's death is evidently a multiple one, and it has its meaning only if we have a relation, in the proper sense of the word, with this other person who is dying. The death of a stranger touches me very little, even though there exists between us the irreducible relation of community in our basic condition; this stranger is, like me, a man. But, in a sense, reduction to this basic relation is so stripped of everything else that it is perhaps literally intolerable. I am too brutally confronted with fundamental human mortality— my mortality—not to be affected by the death of a friend; if I learn of the death of a stranger, it leaves me indifferent. Otherwise, I could not live.

But I can know the other person in a hundred thousand ways: love, friendship, companionship, brotherhood, camping, on a voyage, in a bar, by accident. It is impossible to "make a list" and classify the situations where I encounter the other person, and the ways in which relations are established.

It seems, however, that we can set forth two aspects of the change which the death of the other person introduces into my experience. There is, first of all, the disappearance, the "departure" of this other person inasmuch as he represented to me an important part of my existence. That entails not only very ambivalent sentiments in which, on very different levels, frustration and aggressiveness are mixed, but also the insoluble question of *knowing,* which is commonly called the suffering of mourning.

But the no less insoluble question of my own death also arises, by an irrepressible process of identification. The other person dies in front of me, and this immediately provokes the thoughts: "What about me? When? How?" Such thoughts are immediately rejected in a "don't think of it" attitude, and in the agitation which follows death. "Life has to go on"—a banal expression, whose dramatic intensity resides in the words, "has to," a thought both fatalistic and defensive.

One day, on the road to Lyon, I suddenly came upon a serious accident which had occurred several hundred yards ahead of me, in the right lane. Two powerful cars had collided head-on, at full speed, and I never knew why. On the embankment were the corpses of two men which had been dragged out of the smashed vehicles in the middle of the road and partially covered with blankets. Contrary to what happens during a war, for example, we do not expect to encounter a dead man in this circumstance. First of all, we feel surprised, and the surprise is a disagreeable one because there are dead persons; the spectacle is "not at all pretty."

If we try to analyze our emotions in these circumstances, it is clear that what dominates is the threat by identification. The other person who is dead and whom I see is a stranger. This is the first time that I meet him. And it is only because he is dead that I meet him. If the accident had not taken place, our paths would have parted twenty or thirty miles from there, and I would never have known him. I suddenly learn of his existence because I see him dead. My relation to him is really reduced to very little; I *see* him dead, and in circumstances very similar to mine, since I also am in a car, and on the same road. In other words, I am directly threatened with an accident.

It would be quite hypocritical and illusory to think that my dominant emotion is pity. Actually, it is first of all identification and fear. And even when I begin to think of the dead stranger as a subject and of all those who will be touched by his death, I still can do it only by way of identification. I will think first of all of his wife or of his children according to my own affective prevalences.

All of this is so true that—and these are well-known reactions—as I continue my voyage, I will drive more slowly and be more attentive, for ten miles or so, for as long as it takes for the vision to fade, and I will regain my composure by telling myself, much in the manner of a magical conjuration, "An accident happened on this road today. There isn't much chance that another will take place, or that it will happen to me!" This is as stupid as is the famous "never two deaths without a third," which is supposed to signify the inverse.

It happens to every man that, when he reaches a certain age, he one day "loses his father." This is a very particular event.

Quite evidently, what predominates here is the abrupt change in a long established and developed intersubjective relationship. Identification also comes into play, assuredly, but it is inscribed in an entire process which psychoanalysis has brought to light, and it is, in a way, only one stage in this process.

When all goes well, the son progresses in his own consciousness of himself as a man according to a difficult ambivalence in relation to the man who is there, joined to his mother, and whose word is law. We will not spend more time on the details of this evolution which generally resolves itself when the Oedipus crisis is passed, and then in the assumption of interior autonomy which inaugurates adolescence.

In a way—and we are stating things only very schematically—it was necessary for the son to "kill" his father, in a sense, in order to be, according to a dialectic of aggressiveness and guilt which resolves itself in balanced filial love.

He had to "kill" the "ideal father"—who did not exist, as everyone knows—and the "imaginary father," who did not exist either. Characters in the child's affective world of phantasms, these "fathers" were developed or known according to the child's lived experience with the man-who-is-there, but whom he could not yet know. It is precisely in accepting the desirable "death" of these characters that the son can finally know the *real* father, disengaged sufficiently from phantasms and ambivalence to be at least perceived. This corresponds to his integration into his own personal duration; he can perceive himself as a *future* father. That is to say, real duration implies for him that his real father is mortal.

When his father dies, all of the son's affective world is directly concerned. The relation changes radically: the real father no longer manifests himself, and the son must be able to go beyond these manifestations.

In a sense, this establishes, once and for all, true solitude —that is, autonomy. But it is quite rare that this evolution takes place in conditions so favorable that the passage is made somehow "quite naturally." Usually, there remain in the son some significant traces of the relational ambivalence of childhood and of adolescence. The "symbolic murders" were not entirely assumed and resolved; aggressiveness and fear subsist more or less in the obscure zones of the son's personality. This can condition paradoxical reactions: stoic "courage," panic, collapse, cynicism—which for some time surprise those who surround the son.

But knowledge of the real father by the son ends there— in the sense of "is completed"—because the father is not only imagined mortal, but also "lived dead." The son can then complete his identification and feel himself fully man—that is, father and mortal. When all has happened normally, the father's death is a solemn and ultimate moment in the son's maturation. But, obviously, the primitive conflicts must have been resolved in at least some kind of a satisfying manner.[1]

In the case of a spouse's death, it is in like manner the "disappearance" of the other person which predominates, and identification with his mortal condition is only indirect. If the couple's relationship was positive and "successful"—that is,

[1] We offer only one example here, in order not to make this chapter too heavy. It is clear that the death of a mother resounds in a very different way in the affective obscurity.

if they really loved one another—frustration and rupture are dominant. Popular language once again translates well the intensity of the event, as well as the radical impossibility of expressing it adequately: "I have lost half of myself." Furthermore, this tends to place the survivor in a vaster reality; actually, it is the couple which has lost one of its "halves." Instead of being a promotion to autonomy, the death of a beloved spouse can only be irreparable frustration, a definite loss, without "compensation."

Let us note, in passing, the strange "contradiction" in love. When it takes place, it abolishes, in a way, the notion of duration or at least that of fading away, and strongly so. We "set out for life" with the impression that it will last "forever," and this "forever" avoids the implication that it means "until death." "Forever" for us means a "duration without end"; thus there is instinctive flight from the reality of duration, which is precisely that it does end.[2]

In any case, the death of the beloved spouse is felt as a loss, a "lack," which, unlike the death of a father, does not open up to a call to live a fuller existence. Among some old couples, we see that when one dies, the other seems to take on little by little an attitude of existence which is nothing but a waiting. Some even say as much: "I have nothing left to do but to join her." This signifies first of all a more immediate acceptance of his own death, but also the irrepressible sentiment of an "elsewhere," as vague as it may be, even in this expression of apparent annihilation: "I have nothing left to do but to join her in death." We do not *join* anyone in *nothingness*.

I once had occasion to follow closely for several weeks a situation that undoubtedly was not an exceptional one. A

[2] It is not rare for a man who knew great love to remarry some time after the death of his wife, and to experience another great love, perhaps as profound although radically different, without, however, *forgetting* or annihilating the first. Experience shows that this occurs —seemingly more so for a widower than for a widow. The question of the human couple is a very strange one; it is simultaneously so *total* and so *relative*.

fifty-year-old woman died of cancer. Her husband, who lived with her and who cared for her with great gentleness, had installed his mistress in his place of business. Nevertheless, when his wife died, the emotion and mourning which he manifested were not false, but they were transitory. Even in this case, a relationship of communion of life had been established, and, according to popular language, it "did something to him nevertheless." Perhaps this man was just trying unconsciously to hide from himself the finity of duration.

Different again is the situation created by the death of a child. The underlying affective implications are perhaps more important here, and very complex. The death of a son or a daughter will not be felt in the same way by the father and by the mother, and this depends on the projections, compensations, suppressed aggressiveness, etc. of which the child could have been the object or occasion.

But in a general way, we can say that the parent is frustrated at losing a kind of future on which he had counted. It is easy to conceive, for example—to mention the most typical kind of situation—that a lawyer whose only son is a law student would have no more "reason to live" if this son, who was to continue after his father and be his extension in time, were to die while he is still a student.

Even in situations which are less clear, the death of a child always involves this anticipated break, this "upset in duration," this "lack of logic in nature," which suddenly faces parents with the black emptiness of the rupture. They are violently frustrated to lose a dimension of themselves—a "signification forward," we might say, and confrontation with their own finiteness results from this particularly dramatic event.

We could, of course, mention other situations—e.g., the death of a mother or the death of a friend—but the infinity of affective relationships cannot be imprisoned in a catalogue.

In any case, the death of the other beloved person constitutes an experience of change in the relation to this other person, of which certain aspects should be emphasized. We will not insist upon the *normal* ambivalence of the relation to the other person (which is where agony arises, in the psycho-analytical sense of the term). Freud's analysis of the function of mourning places it in sufficient light. But it is on this basic conditioning that the relation unfolds. And it is not without interest to note that psychoanalytical knowledge of man shows the radical incompleteness of love, and its return to what we call hatred and the desire to murder. Long before the time of psychoanalysis, and in the mode of a mythical tale, Genesis told the story of Cain and Abel.

When the other beloved person dies, the one who survives is introduced to a radically new mode of *positive* relation: that of *absence*. Absence is a mode of presence, and not at all an annihilation. Absence, literally, is "existence-not-here," the existence "elsewhere" of something or someone—an existence, if we may so express it, which turns its back and looks else-where.

It would be interesting to reflect on the mode of presence that absence is. Two examples can serve this reflection; they are apparently very different, but they are really very closely linked by their symbolic significations.

For a mutilated person, the member which he has lost is in a sense more massively and more continually present to him than if he still had it. Consciously or with the automatism of habit, he has to "take account" *positively* of the absence of his member and of modes of compensation, and this in a continual and definitive manner. Paradoxically speaking, we can say that a member is more *encumbering* when it has been cut off. But this "presence of lack," if it is assumed, can be literally the promotion of certain virtualities in the subject, which would not have been revealed without the mutilation, even, simply, on a professional plane. And in this case it can very well be a matter not of compensation, but quite literally of promotion.

This is also connected with the profound reality of fun-damental and primitive "loss" which psychoanalysis brings to light in the most primitive upheaval of subconscious life.[3] By its continually present lack, the primitive and obscure "object lost" stimulates the evolution and progress of what will be the unexpressible unicity of the consciousness of a *subject*.

The other example is that of separation. Let us take the case of the person who remains while the other beloved person —spouse, friend, son—is absent for a rather long time. A kind of purification takes place; the little faults, the inevitable reasons for impatience, instances of lack of understanding— all fade away and wither. The other person begins to live in his positive reality more than in his negative aspects. But at the same time, he becomes a question: "What is he doing? Is he having difficulties? Is he thinking of me?" He lives with all the more intensity. And we suppose that it is reciprocal— that is, that the other person, also, from his side, knows the same purification and anxiety.

Separation—absence—is, like every lived reality, ambivalent. It enables love or affection to be deepened by stripping it of the "clouds" of daily existence. But it includes the danger of insidiously replacing the real other person with an ideal image which we make of him according to the desire we have. But in any case, absence is not annihilation—quite the contrary.

According to an old song, "To leave is to die a little." We can say that "to die is to leave completely." But to leave does not signify to no longer be; it signifies merely to no longer be *accessible*. Nothing permits us to affirm anything else with regard to "departure" in death.

In the relation to the other beloved person, this departure introduces the new situation of "presence by definitive absence." The other person is no longer here in a common duration. His presence is inscribed in the mode of purification and anxiety, but without any possible return.

It is striking to see how much those who die cease to have faults and suddenly reveal so many good qualities that we had

[3] Cf., by the same author, *Mystère humain de la sexualité*. Editions du Seuil.

not noticed. Even when a very wicked person dies, he appears with a mysterious "human core," with a "possibility of being man" which was hidden up to then.

In a sense, we can say that this definitive presence-absence of death places the other person in an authentic reality of himself, and strips away insufficiencies, oddities and incompletenesses. We discover the thousand traces of the dead person furnished by objects, old photographs, various papers, etc., sometimes long after his death. We understand attitudes and reflections which we did not understand while he "was here." We forgive, eventually, and we perceive that there was not even anything to forgive. The reality of the other person, departed thus "forever," is, if we reflect on it, singularly more consistent in this "distance" taken definitively and without possible return to confusion or misunderstandings. And this reality of the other person is especially free from any possessiveness; since he is no longer here, we no longer have him "at our service." Forgetfulness, when it begins to establish itself, is only apparent. Actually, the presence of the departed person is irrepressible; it is merely masked by the realities of duration which continue for the person who remains. Suffering also lessens; but if we reflect on it, it can be attenuated— absence being "tolerated"—only because the other person is not annihilated. Often it is difficult enough to accept the fact that he is no longer accessible; spiritist invocations, in their lamentable illusion, furnish proof. But where is this "place of the dead" where those whom we loved dwell?

Every relation is reciprocal. This means that the person who remains says to himself, for example, "Now he understands me better; he knows that a certain aspect of me is not deeply rooted; he knows that I loved him better than I could ever make him understand; he 'sees.'"

I think that even if we deny it (because of pride or some philosophical *a priori*), every human being who lives through the agony of the death of another beloved person reacts *spontaneously* in this way. Why, then, deny it?

What we call memory, in the expression "keep a memory

of the departed," is really a new mode of knowledge, and therefore of relation, unexplorable and not able to be analyzed in itself. After all, it is not paradoxical to say that death introduces persons to a reciprocal presence in which the daily obstacles to coexistence in time and the dialectical tension in every relationship are resolved, and *solitude* disappears. It is necessary to die to be truly *together*.

When we truly love someone, we are anxious about him, and we cannot even consider the annihilation of his being. Whatever his age and however the other beloved person may have died, it can only be an interruption. In other words, it is an insurmountable impossibility for him to realize what still remained for him to realize—and which is, in fact, indefinite. Even an old man makes plans, and a sick man whom you know has only two months to live will speak to you of next year and where he intends to spend his vacation. The person we love never "stops existing"; the worst suffering is perhaps knowing that he does not have long to live, and desiring nevertheless— because we love him—that he could have been happy realizing what, now, can never materialize for him. This frustration-for-him of death is unacceptable. The militant Communist whose father gave his life to establish a better world without having seen it established cannot tolerate the thought that his father will not know the realization of his hope.

The death of the other beloved person poses, in every way, this fundamental question—an insidious one, impossible to elucidate: "What is there *for him* of his "will to be?" We can surmount deceived hopes, with difficulty, but is the deceived hope of a person whom we truly love tolerable?

I remember an occasion when I felt very deep emotion. It was a morning in September 1945. I had been called back to active duty as an army doctor, and I was stationed with my unit in a little Alsatian village while waiting to leave for the Far East. Nearby in the countryside, there was a small military cemetery containing the bodies of soldiers who had died during the reconquest of Strasbourg. I discovered it one morning while I was taking a walk. According to the dates written on them, nearly every cross seemed to cry out, "I died when I was only twenty years old."

A man who dies at the age of twenty! Whether we know him or not—independently of family relations, of course— the death of a young man is always disturbing. But why?

First of all, I think that we feel ourselves concerned by the way that the sense and value of duration are put into question; they are somehow *denied* by such an event. We can also have a feeling of "guilty conscience" when we compare the frustration which the other person has undergone, almost before he got started, in this "thing" which is life and which, on the other hand, we enjoy with some comfort.

We can think, however, that after all, this young man who died was fortunate, because if life involves joys and discoveries, it also involves threats of terrible sufferings, which *last*. Looking at a young twenty-year-old who fell onto a mine, whose two legs and an arm have to be amputated, and who will be blind for life, the surgeon really asks himself whether it might be better for him to die rather than for decades to endure the existence of "human debris." And yet, if every overly abnormal child had to be allowed to die or had to be "put out of his misery" under the pretext that he would have too much to suffer, wouldn't it be necessary to go so far as to *kill* every child of whom we could not know beforehand whether he would contract polio, be a prisoner of war, tortured, abandoned, or be the victim of a cruelly unfaithful wife?

This brings to mind the rich man who has a Jaguar and who says to the little worker who has nothing but an old jeep: "You do not know how fortunate you are! These English cars are fragile, and they are always giving a person some kind of trouble. If I could, how quickly I would take your place!"

However, it seems to me that the death of a young person brings us to quite another level, and a very fundamental one —the level of sexuality. In this regard, some readers will undoubtedly think that we are returning to Freud's "pansexualistic obsession"—perhaps because they are defending themselves from their own agonies. But in fact, we now are well aware of the importance of sexual duality in the evolution of the personality.

The death of a young person reaches us all at the level of our most obscure sexual frustrations or agonies, because these frustrations and agonies—very diverse, of course—are inscribed very early in life, and they persist, while they evolve and are partially resolved, in the subconscious life even of those who have best "succeeded" in their existence. When someone dies at the age of sixty, we find it sad because he was "still young." But at least he was able to fulfill himself; he knew the joy of marriage and family life.

The graves in my little Alsatian cemetery made me think of how most of these boys were frustrated by losing the sexual realization, in the broad sense, for which they could all have hoped. And there were undoubtedly a few religious or seminarians among them. In this respect, the death of a young person is undoubtedly related to the conflict of castration, so complex and of diverse symbolic levels, which psychoanalysis has brought to light.

When an important political leader dies, the reactions of the crowd are very symptomatic. And what dominates is undoubtedly an obscure sentiment of insecurity, while a feeling of liberation is outlining itself fatally—and not without an underlying uneasiness—in another part of the population. One man asks, "What will happen now that he is no longer here?" Another will answer, "We can finally have a change." But the basic uncertainty of each is the same, and it is eventually increased by reciprocal fear.

Each person feels the event of death at a certain level, which can be serene enough, and which includes a certain detached attitude. But the obscure, underlying reactions which plunge into the "infantile zones" have a tendency to assert themselves as soon as we are with a crowd of people. There is a kind of cumulative compulsion of emotion which ends up in the "mob reactions" that are well known. And it is difficult to defend oneself from them, so much so that a man, on returning home after a demonstration, can be quite surprised when he remembers the reactions which he just had, and, if need be, the acts in which he just engaged.

It is banal to say that the subconscious affective theme which is dominant here is the theme of the "father" incarnating authority in the ambivalent sense of the term: protection-constraint. But it is interesting to note that, at least for the way that things have evolved in France, a rather important change is taking place and is increasing, and for which an accessible reference point would be the Revolution.

The death of Louis XVI marked the crossing of a threshold of primary importance. Until then, the father myth assured the stability of a civilization, for better or for worse. But his death was desired, and it was violent. Schematically, the royalists felt it as personal mourning, and at the same time as a sacrilege; the republicans experienced it as a liberation and as vengeance, but also with an underlying agony of "sacrilege." The "murder of the father in order to be able to live" was not merely symbolic here; it was bloody. The cruel period which followed, during which men tore each other to pieces, clearly shows the dramatic confusion that prevailed as a consequence. The "terror" was felt not only by the suspects; it was at the very foundation of the reaction of those who held the power. It is because we are afraid that we make terror reign in order to protect ourselves, as much as possible.

The person and the death of Napoleon were undoubtedly quite different in their significance. But the myth was powerful, and it still remains so on occasion. It does not seem to have been directly "parental." Undoubtedly, this man of exceptional ability incarnated the success—the European success—of a people who had become adult and was imposing itself on the neighboring, "crumbling" monarchies—but he did so by copying them, and by marrying the daughter of one of them.

It seems that, progressively during the 19th century, the reactions of the population on a whole at the death of chiefs of state or of important governors modified themselves considerably. The death of Charles X or that of Louis-Philippe was felt only by a restrained group of faithful followers. Without doubt, the death of Napoleon III was noticed still less.

Certainly, passionate and mythical reactions tend to reappear easily on the occasion of grave, exalting or catastrophic events. All the men of my generation felt the death of Clemenceau, for example, as the end of a period, lived during the course of childhood, and as the disappearance, the "passage into memory," of great fundamental emotions. We could also analyze the death of Pétain, from the viewpoint of the reactions which it provoked. In its totality, the Pétain event is the inverse of the Clemenceau event, in that it has been increasingly catastrophic. Perhaps this explains why, in certain areas of the population, his death was felt—and it still is felt somewhat—more in the mode of mythical regression.

It seems that we can say that civilization's evolution is tending toward a human organization which is ever farther from the "father myth"—in other words, toward a world in which the death of an important leader will be felt in a less emotional manner. In all times and under all regimes, the death of a leader has put into question on different levels a certain "assured duration," a certain "functioning of things." Each one asks himself, at least implicitly, what is going to change and in what sense. And every regime tends to assure a continuity, a minimum stability, which is independent of individual persons. The future mode of continuity will undoubtedly not be the same as that which existed up to modern times, since the death of a leader is no longer felt as intensely as the "death of the father" with all of the underlying ambiguity which this involves.

The power of the myth is hardly attenuated in a world transformed by scientific advances. On different levels, certain persons incarnate it, under the pressure of circumstances, to the point that people forget that they are mortal and cannot bear their decrepitude if it happens. Then there is not so much a question of the other person as a person, but of affective projections which have crystallized on him. It is possible that this is a collective phenomenon of reaction to the more cruel lucidity which science gives to man, in the final count, concerning his contradictory destiny in time. European history of the last 150 years would perhaps be interesting to study in this light. For example, under the ancient regime, the hereditary monarchy gave the illusion of overcoming time; the king died, but not the royalty. This was the meaning of the famous formula, "The king is dead! Long live the king!" Under the influence of various factors, this illusion has fallen; and the illusion of immortality cannot hold its ground in the face of the certitude of our knowledge. The "threat of death" in the modern world is, in fact, more constant and more universal from the very fact of the development of technology. We now fear atomic war, airplane accidents, automobile accidents, etc., and this is a change from crossbows and stagecoaches. The evidence of this irreducible ambivalence of progress is so disagreeable that we refuse to admit it, or we eliminate it by saying "Yes, but you're boring us; it's an old cliché."

Insofar as we know, Stalin's death was hidden for some time; however, even if this is not true, it shows that we could think it was done. For many years, Churchill's decrepitude was concealed, as a recent press investigation has revealed in England. For his faithful, and despite the nomination of a successor, Hitler was immortal, but his realm collapsed in a particularly tragic manner when the illusion was dissipated.

In quite another perspective, it is striking to compare the reactions of the crowd and of people around them to the death of Pope Pius XII and to that of Pope John XXIII. For the first, it is beyond debate that a good many people retreated within themselves in an attitude that refused to accept what was evident; they prayed for his *cure* even though he was "at the end of his time"— not a very Christian *position,* if we reflect on it! The myth undoubtedly had a lot to do with this. For the second, the reaction was very different (and undoubtedly more Christian); they prayed with him to "accompany his passage" and his arrival in the mystery beyond time.

Without doubt, many complex factors came into play to manifest this difference. However, it is nevertheless striking that, in a perspective which is in principle the discovery, in Christ, of the positive meaning of death,[4] people could let themselves be so carried away by the power of the myth of a time without end.

The other person who dies is sometimes a person who made us uncomfortable. We need not deny that this is often the case, although, in a general way, we refuse to admit it. And the situations are infinitely diverse.

In general, the living presence of this other person prevents us from living "fully," or from taking the fullest measure of existence which should be possible. If he were to die, many things would take care of themselves. He may be the superior, who is too old and authoritarian, who slows down or prevents the normal movement of evolution, and who does not see certain new problems. It may be the aging patriarch whose weight is suffocating the whole family, or the senile old grandfather who never manages to die. It may be the clever rival who prevents our advancement. It may be the fifty-year-old proprietor whose house we have bought on the agreement that we will pay rent until his death, and whose rapid departure would be welcome. It may be the person with an incurable illness whose approaching death leads everyone around him to help him in his suffering.

A thousand and one circumstances of concrete life give rise to this strange sentiment, and I believe that no one escapes it. It is so frightening that we misunderstand it or seek to justify it—this desire for the death of another person.

The human conscience is not happy to learn that we are all "subconscious criminals." In a very general and very diverse manner, the desire for the death of the other person participates *subconsciously* in many of our attitudes.

This conclusion by modern psychology often gives rise to

---

[4] We will return to this aspect in the last part of this book.

indignant protestations by people who only see good in others. However, it is strange that the latter forget so completely that the same affirmation is made at the beginning of biblical revelation, because this is the meaning of the symbolic narrative of Cain and Abel.

Most of the time, without realizing it, we fight against this underlying desire for the death of others, in a fundamentally ambivalent reaction which combines the elements of a fear of guilt and—perhaps because of this fear—consideration for the other person—in a word, true love.

When it is a matter of a person close to us, with whom continuous affective relations are established, we cannot admit to ourselves this desire for the other's death which remains in the obscure zones of conflicts that have been more or less overcome. And when we ascertain, for example, that a son desires the death of his only remaining parent in order to secure his inheritance, we spontaneously experience sentiments of disgust, horror and repulsion, which means that this attitude which we see resounds in our own subjective reactions; actually, we are "denying" that we have a similar attitude, which proves that we recognize it as possible. When, on the contrary, it is a matter of a person who is distant from us— with whom our relations are limited to a professional rivalry, for example—we can speak about it. A certain employee will say, "If X . . . would go, it would do a lot to help me to advance." We deny that "go" means anything other than retirement or a change of employment. But easy as it might be to live with X . . . , we will sometimes go so far as to joke, "If he'd croak, what a relief it would be," and everyone laughs, in order to exorcise something.

The desire for the death of the other person is really a bearable attenuation of the desire to *murder* the other person, to murder "by a go-between": an accident, illness, etc. Such a desire to murder we hide as cleverly as we would take the initiative if the culpability were not so intense.

This desire to murder the other person, which is always ready to arise in the affective obscurities of our affective life—

as the Bible proclaims—is usually resolved in a "wish," in a more or less explicit "expectation," felt in a more bearable mode of culpability. It is also resolved in "symbolic murder." Certain virulent critics will say, for example: "X . . . talked to me about Z . . . the other day. He really tore him apart. Nothing was left of him." And a certain underling who has his eye on his immediate superior's position will gladly say that the latter, who is very active, does not spare himself enough, that he is "slowly killing himself"—and he says this with a secret and obscure satisfaction.[5]

It can happen that the desire to murder exists as such in a person's consciousness and conduct. In other words, he experiences the other person as literally intolerable. This can present very varied modalities which we do not have time to examine here. I would like to mention merely two.

One night, a group of delinquent adolescents—"leather jackets," as they are called—attacked an unknown North African and killed him by bashing in his head with cobblestones. Some time later, I was able to speak with one of these boys, one who had not participated actively in the tragedy, but who had been present, in all of the emotional intensity which this implies. It seems that two themes dominated in this group violence. On the one hand, there was a kind of anxious need to see just how far power over life went; this is in line with the attraction to personal danger which leads the adolescent to play with his own existence as though he can prove in this way that he really possesses it. On the other hand, in the context of the Algerian War which was then going on, this poor unknown man represented to them an intolerable "human image" composed simultaneously of decadence and revolt, fully implied in their own personal tragedies. However, the fact was exceptional inasmuch as it did pass into act.

[5] We should not think that modern psychology takes pleasure in morbidness. We did not have to wait until Freud to know that the heart of man is contradictory. I think that it was J. de Maistre who said, "I do not know what a criminal's conscience is; the only conscience with which I am acquainted is that of an honest man, and it is horrible."

The other situation is one which we can modestly call "euthanasia." Whether it concerns an abnormal child or a person with an incurable illness, under the humanitarian—and sincere—excuse of "sparing him from suffering," there is always a hidden desire to make this "object" which has become intolerable disappear—and we offer "good reasons" for doing so.

It is beyond debate that the desire for the death of the other person, rooted obscurely in what we can call the possible rise of the desire to murder, is spontaneously felt as culpable —or, in other words, as a threat. The "Thou shalt not kill" of the decalogue does not belong exclusively to the Judaeo-Christian tradition; we find it, for example, under another form in the Egyptian Book of the Dead.

It is interesting to note that even though murder is so fundamentally condemned by universal human moral conscience, it is nevertheless so widespread in all of its aspects, from crime, to war, to social chastisement. In any event, murder cannot be lived in affective neutrality, or even in a minor mobilization of the emotional life. The "cynicism" which sometimes accompanies it—in certain crimes or in certain collective psychoses such as that of Nazism—dissimulates under an apparently incomprehensible coldness, a confusion and agony which are intolerable and therefore suppressed. It is at the very sources of affective life that we must look for the origin of this culpability. Freud's discovery of subconscious life has enabled reflection to advance on this point.

A first theme, which has now become almost classical, sets forth the importance of the Oedipus rivalry as the first real "conflict." The "murder of the father" with its very complex affective implications as a reality of subconscious life—individual and collective—is too well known for us to insist upon them. Without question, it has a great part to play not only in the reaction to murder and to death, but also in the primitive structuration of what we can call "religious sentiment"—or rather, "sacred fear"—in the most imprecise sense of this term, and without prejudicing its later content. But it seems that we can go deeper than this.

The progressive structuration of the conscious personality begins with a radical break—that is, a loss or a "fault." If, at the time of his mirror stage, the child begins to take consciousness of himself as a distinct subject, it is because he has been projected into existence by a rupture which, from the very beginning, marks his mode of being in his relation to the other person. Properly speaking, he is *torn* from his mother, and *cut off* from her. Without this primitive drama, as we may call it, we could not properly speak of "him." Very recent research in the perspective of psychoanalysis shows clearly to what point this first experience of a kind of autonomy marks, in its fundamental fact as well as in its ever variable modalities, the existential and affective evolution of each one of us. Indeed, birth takes place in two stages. The child is first of all separated from a part of his own biological being: the membranes, placenta and umbilical cord. Then, that which he abandoned of himself, and *from which he was cut* so that he might live, is, in a second stage, expelled and separated from the biological being of the mother.

We all enter the world by losing, strictly speaking, a part of ourselves, which was an integral part of our previous mode of being. The *loss* of an "object"—which we can call narcissistic in the technical sense of this term—unavoidably conditions our existence. This is an "object" which we will never "recover." Psychoanalytical knowledge shows us that this theme of loss, of break, of chasm, will dominate the subject's entire evolution, with the modal differences which sexual duality introduces and which itself has a sense of break.[6]

In a sense, our subconscious life is obsessed, if we may use the term, with looking for this "object," or with nostalgia for a completeness. And it is precisely this "lack," lived as such

[6] In the Bible, one of the creation narratives (Gen. 2, 21) presents woman to us as fashioned from a rib taken from man, *cut* from him according to the surgical mode of ablation.

in a continual tension and in a continual search, which makes us be ourself, as a distinct subject whose consciousness is structured around this chasm which always cries out in us.

The "lost object"—whose symbolic expressions will be varied indefinitely and developed progressively during the course of life—is held by the "other person." The other person, in the most vague sense of the term, is the "not me." The other person is the one who looks at me, with his incomprehensible interrogation and with his secret, and whose voice reaches me, alternating with silence, like an object which detaches itself and "fall's from one's lips." And to the other person whom I meet—whoever he is—I am the other person.

Thus a reciprocal "question" underlies every interhuman encounter: Does he have what I am lacking? Does he want to take from me something of the most secret part of my substance?

Nor should we forget that at a primitive moment in our lived experience we have *all* been confronted with the desire for our mother (or for her equivalent), and this required that we draw out from ourselves something—from the most unexplorable reaches of ourselves—which cut itself off from us and which we offered to her to satisfy her. With regard to psychological life, this is the real sense of the so-called "anal" period, in which the young child becomes conscious of his sphincteral mastery in terms of the "desire for the other person."

Fear and aggressiveness are always at the heart of every encounter, at least as an ever present virtuality. Why should it be surprising if this aggressiveness is unchained and explodes so often in murder, with the fundamental agony of definitive frustration and culpability? It would not be paradoxical to define civilization—or culture—as the collective effort of human groups to fight against vertigo, to survive it despite everything, by limiting destruction and by suppressing under social organization the ever recurring global wars. It is almost unbelievable to think that our modern Western world, which pushes this anxiety so far as to abolish capital punishment, is at the same time the world where the wholesale killing of two world wars took place, and where the threat and fear of still more spectacular killing remains a menace. And when we reflect on the matter, these killings are always *irrational*: the "goods" which we reciprocally try to tear away from each other or to retake are essentially illusory and a "side issue," whether they be material or ideological. The dramatic history of Nazi Germany illustrates this with unequalled vigor.

This ambivalent vertigo for the "death of the other person," which resounds in the culpability of and confrontation with "one's own death," an ambivalent vertigo of desire and fear, is a fundamental and constitutional factor of human reality.

We did not have to wait for psychoanalysis to be conscious of this. Certainly, until the time of Freud, we merely remained on the level of perception—intense but superficial perception —of the fact. But the Freudian discoveries only elucidated upon the most profound expressions of this reality.[7]

The biblical episode of Cain and Abel, for example, well expresses the agony and drive to murder which revelation connects to humanity's refusal to hear the Word of God.

A short digression suggests itself here to our reflection. Why are words and phrases of condolence always so embarrassing to pronounce, and so solemnly near to the ridiculous? In the face of a person who has lost someone, we find ourselves caught between the necessity of expressing something to him and the impossibility of really doing it. We willingly substitute a silence and a more or less stereotyped mimicry.

It is the very diverse and very embarrassing problem of our reaction in the face of the other person for whom the

[7] Perhaps this is what we forgive the least in Freud and what awakens the most intense resistance to psychoanalysis, without our saying it. I do not think that it is entirely incorrect to say that if psychoanalysis makes people so afraid, this is less because it confronts us with the sexual mystery than because, in the final analysis—and even to make a way for sexuality—, it confronts us, without escape, with the mystery of death and murder.

other person is dead. There is a radical impossibility to "put ourselves in his place," or a threatening danger of overdoing it. We are involved in an event of which an entire side is unexplorable. And since we are not personally concerned by this event—except in the universal dimension of mortality —our best defense is indifference. Faced with the unexplorable, we retreat. I remember two clergymen who encountered each other in a hallway, one of whom learned from the other that the latter had lost his mother eight days before. The confrère, with a tired sigh, answered, "I'll pray for her," which meant, in reality, "What the hell do I care!"

This defense by means of indifference does not make words any easier. If my best friend were to lose his wife, this would touch me, and I would let it touch me. But I would say nothing, because it would be useless to do so, and my words would be so banal as to be almost injurious. If one of my colleagues at the office were to lose his wife, I would express my condolences to him. Social convention admits banalities in this case. If he loses a shrewish, burdensome, half-senile mother-in-law, will I tell him that I am glad for him that he is finally rid of her? "Such is not done," people say. But why not? What appearance has to be saved? More than anything else, what prevents me is a kind of magical fear of being punished if I rejoice at someone's death, even if unrelated to the desire for this death. And if I clearly say what I think, I will do so only with a somewhat provoking cynicism.

We have to admit that we cannot really rejoice at the death of someone who, for example, has lived and suffered for a long time, except in a perspective in which we are persuaded that his death means that he has finally attained the fullness and peace of another life. Outside of this perspective, our embarrassment is total. And yet, how is it that so many Christians do not rejoice for the dead in this way? Is it because they cannot love?

This brings us to ask ourselves another question. In different ways, the death of the other person or the desire for the death of the other person gives rise to diverse emotional re-actions; but in the last analysis, it is all organized around a more or less central pivot: fear of one's own death. Whether we deny it or not, everyone "fears death." But, looking closer, we can ask whether this fear has sense.

In the precise sense of the term, I can fear only a danger or threat which I can, to a degree, imagine. There are no situations in time which, as uncertain or imprecise as they may be, do not involve a possible margin of imagination in refer-ence to experiences lived, even if, at first sight, they are un-related. If, during the course of a voyage, I fear falling into the hands of cruel savages, it is because I carry the knowledge of a certain number of previous such happenings in my psycho-logical baggage.

But death is confrontation with the totally unimaginable. Strictly speaking, we cannot fear death; we can fear the un-known, but outside of the case of death, we fear rather the uncertainty of what will happen and the imaginary aspects connected with it, without knowing what will occur or how. For death, there is nothing; it does not even contain the un-certain, but rather the totally inconceivable. We cannot *fear* something of which we cannot even form the least idea. Every representation of an "afterward," frightening or reassuring, is totally inadequate—and, I would say, useless—because it can only be in and according to time which is our modality of being. And death is precisely the cessation of time.

When someone says, "I am afraid (or I am not afraid) of death," this means, "I am afraid (or not afraid) of being dead"—that is, of being in a situation in which we imagine finding ourselves. And this little sentence signifies implacably that we conceive of ourselves as "existing as dead." We can in no way fear or not fear a situation which we cannot at all imagine.

In reality, it is not death that we fear; rather, we fear dying—that is, "what we feel when it happens." Clearly, we can fear that it will be "painful." It sometimes happens that someone dies peacefully in his sleep, but this is usually an exception. Generally, the person who dies is not comfortable; he suffocates, gasps for air, struggles, wants to speak without being able, cries. If he is in a coma, he moans. And we ask ourselves, more or less clearly, whether we will have the good fortune not to suffer. In fact, it is the only question which preoccupies us in what we call fear of death: "How will it happen to me?" But, strictly speaking, we cannot *fear* death in itself, death as the cessation of time, because it is totally beyond any representation.

Mr. Dupont breathes his last. He is washed and placed on a bed to await the undertaker. From this moment on, we no longer know how to refer to him. As Bossuet said, what lies there on the bed "does not have a name in any language."

We use circumlocutions. If neighbors call, we ask them if they want to see "him." It is evidently not Mr. Dupont, because he *is no longer here*. And yet, it has something to do with Mr. Dupont, or we would in no way be preoccupied with it.

The technical term by which it is designated is "cadaver," but this word is not expressed. We do not invite the neighbors to see "the cadaver." The most we will accept is that the undertaker propose to transfer the "corpse" to the funeral parlor. But we would prefer to say the "casket," getting around the difficulty of speaking about the content by speaking about the container.

We say, "poor Dupont," which does not exactly designate the thing on the bed. Besides, such a designation is purely gratuitous; there is nothing to prove that it is not he who has found true richness.

In conversations, we get around the difficulty by omitting to speak of it. "Mr. Dupont died in his home. The funeral will take place at the church of . . . ." No one thinks of specifying by what means, by what course, and at what moment this encumbering thing, which must be disposed of as soon as possible because of the odor, was transported from one point to another. "The burial will take place at the cemetery of . . . ."

Something is put into the ground, but we cannot manage to say what. In any case, *it is not Mr. Dupont;* everyone agrees on this point.

If it concerns an important or official person, we sometimes say, "The mortal remains will be transferred"—a magnificent and ever so simple expression. Mr. Dupont, when he died, got rid of his remains. They were a nuisance to him, like an old suit of clothes that we like but that we can no longer wear. He goes away and leaves them here, ready to rot and disintegrate. In friendship to him, in "remembrance"—remembrance is a mode of *presence*—we will take care of "them" properly, because "they" belonged to him. It seems to me that this is the adequate term. It puts things in their places, doing away with magical fear and justifying burial honors. And it is easy to conceive of burning these remains, in order to reduce the volume of encumbrance. It is not only rubbish that we burn; we also burn sacred things which we cannot conserve.

Except in answer to the professional needs of medical studies, cadavers are things which should disappear reasonably soon. A cadaver has no sense. There is nothing that is such a nuisance as things which have no sense. And if it happens that a cadaver comes back into circulation as a result of stipulations in a will, it is felt as an incongruity hard to bear.

Not long ago, I assisted at the transferal and "unpotting" of a respectable lady who had succeeded, according to the clauses in her will and historical circumstances, in giving a trip across the country to Paris, fifteen years after her death, to this "thing in a box" which was no longer even a cadaver. In order to insert it into the Parisian vault, it had to be taken out of the too large country casket and placed into a smaller container (the operation which constitutes the "unpotting," in French undertakers' technical language). And what I saw during this process did not have much to it—in other words, nothing but a rather dirty skeleton. Where, then, was the lady? She had spent her life complicating other people's lives;

it is not surprising that she did it again fifteen years after her "departure." Although they tried to hide their feelings, everyone present felt that this time she had exceeded all limits.

Mr. Dupont breathes his last. The most disturbing thing about this unexpressible passing is the fact that his look *disappears*. I purposely say *look,* because even if he no longer sees, if he has lost consciousness without closing his eyes, he still looks. And suddenly, he looks no more; the eyes remain open, but *he looks* no more.

> "Blue or black, all beloved, all beautiful,
> The eyes that are closed can still see."

But where is the look that says more than words, the expressive presence, the reality of the other person toward me, the strictly singular secret of the other person who dies? We cannot throw off this question without an answer. What becomes of him? In what mode of inaccessible being has the "I" which he signified taken refuge?

Whatever the orientation and development of a culture may be, everything is, in fact, always dominated by duration —that is, by a dynamism of development and amelioration which unfolds and proceeds. And at the same time, everything is always dominated by the ever open question of death.

With regard to death, some currents of thought and some civilizations react in rather different ways. In the battle to live, man does not know ultimately how to integrate this contradictory certitude of his death.

The Nazi movement offers the strange case in which a handful of delirious men, carried to power by a dramatic convergence of circumstances, dragged an entire people into a vertigo characterized by the most archaic mythical powers. And everywhere in the world, men and women who belonged to other cultures could be found who were dragged along in this delirium. Fest's very interesting book, *The Masters of the*

Third Reich, clearly shows the truly psychiatric and incoherent aspect of the Nazi push. Death held a preponderant place in this mystique of race—the death of the other person, first of all: the "non-Aryans," but also one's own death. The vertigo of suicide or sacrifice to the Hitlerian idol truly ravaged. Under the appearances of juvenile and dominating power, wasn't it basically a matter of a real mystique of despair?

Apparently stranger and more rational, the Marxist concept of man ends up *not taking account* of death as a fundamental element of reality. Such a fact seems incredible, but nevertheless it is true. I once had occasion to participate in a seminar in which a Marxist offered his contribution in regard to the problem of death. He was an older man, very superior intellectually, culturally, and in quality of conscience. First in listening, then in discussing, I was astounded to realize that he was, in fact, avoiding the question. "Marxism," he told us, "does not have a viewpoint on death."

In his discourse, two themes appeared to be dominant. First of all, there was the strange idea that man develops and *is completed* in commitment *instantaneously*. This amounts to avoiding, right from the beginning, the dialectic of being and time, which is the very contradiction, the insoluble one, that of real human life. The most surprising thing is to see an adult react in this way. Such a reaction is the same as that of the adolescent who has not yet succeeded in integrating his personal duration, his time lived—that is, his death. A former "leather jacket" told me one day, "Up until now, I was able to live only for the moment; now I feel a need to rethink my past in order to form an idea of what I will become." To live for the moment: in other words, in an immobilized consciousness, fixed somehow on a present uneasiness, incapable of assuming what follows and resolving this tension in dreams. This undoubtedly explains the impression we sometimes get when we hear a discourse that is truly Marxist; we waver between its passionate utopia and the implacable and endless unfolding of a logic that is strangely abstract and "intellectualistic." I myself have very often been surprised to see the resemblance between a discourse by a Marxist theorist and one by one or another scholastic philosopher. We feel the same undefinable discomfort which comes from our admiration for the intellectual and verbal play, on the one hand, and, on the other, we feel the annoyance from always being "off to the side of the question." In both cases, there is an impossibility—in the affective order, I think—of integrating and assuming this "personal event which is not an event," this question concerning *one's own* death. All of this undoubtedly happens beneath possible consciousness of it, which accounts for the tenuous and passionate aspect that a discourse by either often takes.

Pushed to ever more ultimate stands during the course of the discussion, our speaker ended up by telling us, in substance, "Historical death does not embarrass us, but I am obliged to admit that personal death does." In the last analysis, that, after all, is *the* question. By "historical death" he meant the death of other persons in the past or future, but as collective entities—that is, abstracting from the reality of agony. And Marxism, since it does not integrate the agony of the insoluble, "does not have a viewpoint on death, because it does away with the intolerable question from the very beginning."

The second theme was closely connected to the first. This discussion took place with Christians, and a very simple opposition was apparent in both the discourse and the discussion which followed: the Christians accepted the idea that they needed someone to complete them, whereas the Marxist passionately and scornfully rejected this "admission of weakness" and "need for another." Here, again, we could not help thinking of the normal oppositional crisis of adolescence, with its need to reject the parental figure and its weight.

I do not believe that it is paradoxical to say that the Marxist reaction to the "problem of death," independent of the tragic sincerity and the crying honesty of such a position, expresses a kind of adolescent agony which does not manage to find a solution in a confrontation with the endless complexity of the real end of duration. We must therefore, in turn, be careful not to fall into a poorly controlled affective reaction. Naiveté is annoying, especially the kind which insists on doing away with duration and death, and it annoys, because in itself it is not sure and *tranquil,* to the degree that we have satisfactorily integrated our own mortal duration as an absolute incertitude of what "non-time" may be. Confronted by a convinced Marxist (or by an impermeable scholastic), it would not take much to bring us to the violence which a fifteen-year-old boy seeks to provoke when he reasons as far as he can see "on the side of life."

Still more naive is what I might call the "American reaction," at least such as it is described by numerous witnesses. A recent film—*Ce cher disparu*—furnished a caricatural description, and caricature does nothing but exaggerate real traits.

We might say that it is not a matter of revolt and denial as in the Marxist protest. It is a matter, in summary, of "playing as though it were not true." Special funeral homes take the cadaver and "treat" it. Embalming, makeup, and staging try to mask the reality of death. One of my friends was invited to a strange cocktail party; a lady was dead, and her children had sent her to a funeral establishment; the night before the burial, the cadaver, prepared, painted, and propped up with bandages and iron rods under her clothing, served as a hostess in greeting the guests in the main parlor, seated in a stuffed chair with a glass in her hand. I think that I would have found this much more macabre and difficult than persons filing in front of a casket. But sensitivities and cultures are so diverse!

We can, nevertheless, ask ourselves what kind of pitiful and naive idealism is hidden under such practices. Is "Americanism," in a different way than Marxism, also a manifestation of the human difficulty to integrate the dialectic of duration and death, to situate it and to give it its meaning?

CHAPTER SIX

The Christian Vision of Death

If the reader has taken the pains to follow me this far, I will ask him now for a final effort at sympathy and comprehension. Without going too far, we can say that Christian faith consists in faith in Christ who saves and resurrects. In other words, the Christian vision of the world and of man is above all a certain way of "living" death by faith in someone.

Following the reflections which have brought us to this point, we cannot help but be confronted with this Christian vision, just as the latter cannot help but be put into question, or help but put into question the human perception of death.

The pages that follow are in no way even a simple outline of a "tract" on "original sin" or the "last ends." In accepting the Christian perception of death as such, in its deep signification, I merely want to express, as I end this book, a few reflections which are in no way intended to teach, but only to be what they are: reflections, and very fragmentary ones.

Before doing anything else, we must reflect a moment on the words involved, because, at the limiting rupture which constitutes death, language easily capsizes, and while seeming to progress, it falls back into confusion or contradiction.

When we speak of immortality, we mean a mode of existence in duration, but indefinite duration. Tomorrow follows today, the day after tomorrow follows tomorrow, and so forth without rupture, without an observable cessation of individual existence intervening. Such a mode of existence is not theoretically inconceivable, but it is practically unthinkable: it is proper to biological processes to grow, to weaken and to cease, at least inasmuch as individual structures are concerned.[1] As we can see, a consciousness' impossibility to conceive of itself as "non-being" is quite another thing. We cannot properly speak of the "immortality" of the subjective consciousness, but rather of its ineffaceable or indestructible character, because, precisely, while being in duration it transcends it. What gives us our language difficulty is the fact that a human being cannot be conceived of as immortal—that is, durable indefinitely—any more than can any other living being, as well as the fact that, nevertheless, a real human *consciousness,* such as it manifests itself to itself and to other human consciousnesses, perceives itself unavoidably as indestructible.

When we speak of eternal life, we mean quite another thing—that is, as a *conceivable* mode of being, but one that is totally unimaginable and outside the reach of every mental representation. It concerns a being not conditioned by duration. Although we have no experience other than existences in duration, and therefore existences that decay, we have to agree that being and duration are not one and the same notion, and that they are not *necessarily* connected. This exigency is undoubtedly introduced by the impossibility, in which we find ourselves, of conceiving of ourselves as non-being, although we ourselves exist in a duration that ends.

When we speak of survival, we are using a very equivocal term. We use it to designate "what happens beyond death" as well as to designate the situation of someone who has escaped death—by means of a surgical operation, for example. The word which comes to mind, then, by an association of meaning, is that of "survival." In other words, survival is situated before "true" death. Thus Lazarus, who came out of the tomb, had to "re-die" sometime later.

---

[1] The species "perpetuate" themselves, as they say, whereas individuals die. Actually, there is only a difference of rhythm, as enormous as it may be, because species also weaken and disappear.

We still speak of "the other world," the "future world" and the "kingdom to come," according to certain expressions in the Christian liturgy and Scripture, but, there again, language fails. We cannot go beyond the boundary which consists in saying that that "world" *is not* the one we know, that it is *other*. When we call it "future," neither is this adequate, because if "we are not yet there," its very definition is to be outside of duration and outside of any qualification which implies time.

We must never lose sight of this language impossibility; otherwise, we run the danger of returning to images which are really mythological and are difficult for a modern mind to accept. Science has taught us that our expression of what we want to say must be scrupulously accurate.

Having said this, we can ascertain that the "Christian fact" is beyond debate and must be taken into account in the history of thought, when not as an area of confrontation.

Without going any farther for the moment, we understand by "Christian fact" the simple ascertainment that for the last 2,000 years there have been men who have referred themselves to a person named Jesus Christ, who can be located historically, and who they say "was resurrected from the dead," and who, being God, came to "take on" human death in order to overcome it and to bring us to share in his victory. This "Christian fact" is beyond debate, and massive in its various aspects. Its foundations—the divinity of Jesus and his resurrection on the third day, as well as his apparitions which followed—are not derived from scientific or rational argument. The Christian attitude consists in a course which is of an entirely different order, one which is situated far beyond the dimensions of logic or abstraction and which is, properly speaking, *faith* in *someone*.

But this Christian fact has introduced to human thought an entirely new and entirely specific vision of death. Instead of throwing it off as unbearable, instead of disguising or exorcising it by means of myths or magical conjurations,

Christian thought assumes and situates death as the central pivot of every signification, as the essential articulation of human completion in the encounter with someone else who "makes himself like men."

Once this encounter and the absolutely new perspective which it opens have been admitted, death no longer appears as an irreducible opacity, *although, nevertheless, its character as an absolutely radical rupture does not disappear.* In becoming the very center of faith—by the fact of Jesus' violent death and everything that is connected with it—death suddenly appears as the capital event which liberates and which completes each one of us in the perfection of love. To repeat P. Ricoeur's expression, in the Christian vision, death, which we could not truly call an event—because we could only explore one side of it—becomes an event, its signification on the other side being revealed to us. Death then becomes the personal *event* par excellence, and even *accession* to being outside of time.

In this, something happens which we might compare to facts of daily life. If, at night, I enter a street which is lighted only at its entrance, I certainly feel that I am going somewhere, but it is completely impossible for me to see the "other end"; it would be necessary for the electric light company, independently of my desire or my power, to light up the other end of the street.

If we admit the Christian vision, then by means of the enlightenment which another gives us (not philosophically, but existentially and by himself), death reveals itself abruptly as the "explosion" of the "I" outside of the limits of duration and its accession to what we can call, strictly speaking, unimaginable *eternal* existence.

After all, why shouldn't we admit this "Christian vision"? Nothing in modern thought, deeply enriched by scientific knowledge, can bring us to conclude that it is incompatible with what we know, precisely because it is a radically different perception of death, against which scientific knowledge beats desperately, and because it is able to "take up" where scientific reflection "left off." Not by deduction, certainly! There is no common measure between them.

Here, again, I am tempted to make a comparison: although a physician or a biologist "reviews" all of his knowledge, this will not entirely satisfy his desire to live; it is in a woman's look that he will find "what follows."

The same is true of faith, in its own proportions: it is in someone's Word that we find "what follows."

Having learned from his experience at Athens, St. Paul declared to the inhabitants of Corinth that he was not going to speak of highly philosophical and intellectual ideas. He came simply "to announce Jesus Christ crucified," dead and resurrected—someone who is of another order, who is the living God, who lived the most ignoble violent death, to show us where he will lead us if we are willing to follow him and have confidence in him. To arrive at this point, centuries of slow maturation were necessary, because he who revealed himself in this historical drama did not irrupt into it without *foretelling* it.

The first historical manifestation of revelation took place with Abraham, about 1,800 years before the time of Christ. The living God (beyond every name and every image) promised to make a covenant with the tribe—a promise of salvation, perpetuity and expansion. The tribe, as the people whom God addressed, would be victorious over time and death. But it was the tribe as such, and the promise remained on the level of temporal duration conceived of as being without end. In other words, in the primitive Semitic mentality there was no place for the idea of a personal destiny for each person, or for the idea of a human existence outside of time—that is, strictly speaking, eternal.

Other perspectives unfolded only progressively. For ten centuries, evolution was minimal. What counted for the faithful Jew was the salvation of his people and its victory over its enemies. For him personally, if he observed the law, he would live to an old age and in peace, and prosper. After this, it is very vague: he would "rejoin his fathers"; he would go to "scheol," an obscure region, the abode of the dead, a "place of absence." The idea of a personal existence beyond death was, if we may say so, instinctive, but without any other profundity and very obscure.

With Ezekiel, a new element appeared in a formal and solemn way and overturned all of the perspectives. God announced that each man is responsible for himself and must be in dialogue with him. The personal destiny of each man, according to whether he was faithful or not, came to the fore. The context of the tribe was already surpassed; this message was addressed virtually to every human conscience.

But this posed a terrible problem, and the book of Job expresses it. God promised that every just man would have his recompense—that is, he would live to old age, prosper, and be respected, surrounded by the "fourth and fifth generations" of his descendants. But experience cruelly refuted this affirmation. In fact, it was evident that it is the villains who often succeed. (As we can see, the fact is not new!) The just man finally finds himself stripped of everything, and he can no longer understand; this is the whole meaning of the "story" of Job. With unequal accents, the author of the book expresses irreducible suffering and total confusion in face of the injustice of destiny. He does not know how to resolve the terrible question, and he entrusts himself to the unexplainable plan of God who cannot be measured by human thought. And the book ends with Job being reestablished as a rich man. He was faithful in temptation and in face of the incomprehensible, and therefore he was rewarded. But the author does not yet have any other language available, and in order to express what he wants to say, he finds himself obliged to use the symbol of temporal prosperity, which he had nevertheless radically put into question.

The breach, if we may call it that, was opened, by which the idea of personal existence beyond death would be able to impose, affirm, deepen and disengage itself progressively in this primitive perspective of a time without end. Death took

on another meaning. From that time on, and ever more explicitly, it became "liberation," a passage which enables a man
to end up *beyond time* in the realism of his own total person—
which implies an affirmation of the resurrection of the "body."

It is a matter of entering into a *new* world, rid of time and
sin, if we can express ourselves in this strange way, a new
world to which God would introduce us by means of his
"envoy," he who would accomplish the universal covenant.
Isaiah even used an image—to which we will return later:
the world of darkness "will give birth"; in other words, death,
in one of its aspects, appears literally as a *birth*.

By itself, this perspective resulted in exploding the idea
of the salvation and triumph of the tribe. This "new world" is
beyond the successes or failures of time; a man has to die to
reach it. But it is also beyond the limits of every tribe and
every civilization; it is universal, in the very precise sense of
the term.

Until the time of Jesus, this was only a hope, an invincible
expectation. With him, it was a *fact*. This new world beyond
time—which we call the "kingdom of heaven"—was already
there, in his historical presence and its meaning of rupture
and resurrection.

We know how difficult it was for the Jews to accept to
locate this "salvation" outside of the context of their tribe,
traditions and customs. It was one of the elements in Jesus'
condemnation to death. And the first time that the apostles
found themselves back in Jerusalem after having begun to
spread the Good News, a very lively discussion on this subject
took place between Paul, who had crossed this threshold, and
James and Peter, who found it difficult to do so.[2]

When Jesus began to travel throughout Palestine and to
speak publicly, this idea of the resurrection of the body al-

---

[2] It should be noted that this difficulty—renouncing the establishment of a "kingdom" beyond time in time—has always existed and
will not be resolved soon. What has been very correctly called at
Vatican Council II the Church's "triumphalism" is an evident sign of
it. Whether we believe in Christ, whether we "know," we still have a
hard time, right to the end, to *truly* integrate death and its meaning.

ready existed in Scripture, in the book of Maccabees, but not everyone accepted it. Those who shared in the politico-religious structures—the doctors of the law, the Sanhedrin, the "ecclesiastics" of the temple—were rather refractory; they could feel confusedly that it put into sharp focus the question of their "temporalistic" attitude and mentality. The Sadducees, the most "retarded," laughed at it scornfully: what is this invention which is not contained explicitly in the primitive books?

The short controversy which they had with Jesus shows to what degree the realistic idea of death and resurrection had gone beyond the primitive notions. Right from the beginning, we find the Sadducees' argument strangely puerile. For a moment we say, "What? They were still there?" Furthermore, it is significant that the question which they posed concerned the central problem of sexuality and its future.

Another fact shows clearly the total specificity of the Christian idea of death: it is Paul's adventure on the Areopagus. When he spoke of Jesus as "resurrected from among the dead," all of the eminent intellectuals, except one, began to laugh. And yet, the Greek, Roman and Oriental religions all included an "other life," "regions beyond death," and a whole mythology concerning them. But this reaction to Paul's words shows to what point it was imaginary and mythical. The realism of the resurrection of the body surpassed and baffled them. And because they did not understand, they laughed.

The Christian vision of death, centered on the death of Jesus, his resurrection and the "alimentary" sign which he gave of it, is therefore essentially realistic, stripped of all poetry and all imagination: each one of us, by this event which finally makes sense, is stripped of insufficiency, of "sin" and of the consciousness-duration contradiction; we enter, by means of a real mutation, into the mode of existence which is, properly speaking, eternal, and each one of us does this in the totality of his radically renewed *person*. This is where language stops, if we do not want to fall back to the level of mythological imaginings.

Reflections

In the world which is ours, a concept such as death results in numerous questions and numerous remarks. We do not intend to write a "tract on death" here; it would be a ridiculous pretension. But it seems necessary to at least broach certain reflections.

The Christian Vision and Anthropology

Death is a concrete fact, universal and without change, always posing to human consciousness the same question that has no rational answer. However, civilizations and cultures have been very diverse. They have approached this massive and opaque fact in very different ways, extending from scorn to worship, and passing through a multitude of mythological interpretations.

The new fact in the history of human thought is the development, since the 17th century, of scientific methods and knowledge, properly speaking, and of their consequences. In rhythm with the discoveries which this has brought about and rapidly accelerated, everything has come to appear quite different from what it was thought to be up to that time. What we can really call modern cosmology and anthropology have come into existence.

Until that time, the facts of observation were reported by a vision of things which dated back to the ancient authors and received its meaning from them. From the time of the Middle Ages, the focal point of all knowledge was even explicitly theological. It consisted in reading in nature what was already known about creation and of furnishing some kind of explanation for a "given knowledge" whose repercussions were endlessly explored.

Since the 17th century, another mode of knowing, more virtual than explicit up until then, burst forth with considerable force. There was no longer question of "verifying" what is implicitly contained in a "superior" knowledge—philosophical or revealed. It consisted in seeing by oneself, beginning only with observation, reasoning and experimentation, how things happen and how the world is structured. This change in attitude did not take long to provoke a violent conflict with the Galileo affair. Very rapidly, the fact that the scientific discoveries put into question the world-vision established up until then provoked indignation. The minds of the time thought that pretending to know something without worrying about what God or the philosophers had said really amounted to sacrilege, and they could not discern clearly between the truly theological content of thought and contingent applications to knowledge of the world. Attacking the representation of celestial mechanics which had been admitted until then was equated to attacking without distinction the Word of God, the Church and revelation. This undoubtedly surprises us, but we should not lose sight of the fact that scientific knowledge had hardly begun to affirm itself when faced with a philosophico-theological fortress solidly structured and congealed in its structures. It is impossible for us to obtain an idea of how an educated man of the 17th century pictured the world to himself. However, an example may help us to grasp it. Bossuet wrote, in his *Elévations sur les Mystères,* "Woman is nothing but the product of an extra bone." This eminently serious man did not intend this remark as a joke. It means exactly that for him the scientific reference point for anthropology was the biblical text taken literally. It was necessary to wait until the time of Pope Pius XII for it to be finally clearly affirmed that the first eleven chapters of Genesis have theological import with regard to the transcendence of creation, but not an historical and scientific value in the actual meaning of these words.

The conflict between "science" and "faith" is a false conflict, because two radically different orders of knowledge are concerned, different in their modes of knowing and in what they discover. But it is normal for a sometimes violent confrontation to take place between a "theology" which pretends to do the work of biology and a science which pretends to include or give rise to a theology. Confusion between these two domains is far from being dissipated. A theology tributary to a pre-scientific reflection can never manage to situate the exact threshold of its limits, and therefore, of its proper domain; this is the case of some decadent scholasticism. Won't the world to come seek to develop a theology which is more disengaged from these confusions and which expresses itself simply according to categories and in a language which the modern scientific mind can understand?

Our reflection on death could no longer be exactly the same as it was in 16th-century thought, for example. In a simplistic way, I would say that it can no longer appear as a "catastrophic accident," but as the rupture or explosion of a perpetually resurging tension.

Until modern times, the world was pictured as being well ordered. There were "elements." There were inert matter, vegetal life, animal life and man. There were species, genera, and subgroups. The whole was conceived of without real change. In this vision, death could be conceived of only as illogical, a pure accident, unforeseeable and nevertheless strangely fatal. It was personified as an exterior enemy; in a way it was conceived as a heterogenous factor.

During 100 years of historical and paleontological discoveries, the sciences of nature and the sciences of man have modified this vision of the world. The universe appears to us as essentially unitary, in continual expansion, and in continual evolution, according to an immense dynamism that is really asymptotic. Between species, even between kingdoms, we perceive that there is not this solution of apparent continuity. In an unbelievable constructive bubbling, of which we can still perceive only a few reference points in a time that is much more "drawn out" than we believed, the world passes almost imperceptibly from "inert" structure to living structure, and then to "thinking" structure. We can no longer conceive of God as a "manufacturer," as the imagery in Genesis seems to present him to us, if we remain on the superficial level of the text; we are obliged to look deeper, to make a much more transcendent picture of the creator, an uncomfortable picture because we cannot grasp it and "walk around it." And this dynamism surging in perpetual succession tends to the intemporality of consciousness by dashing itself against the fact of death—that is, the apparent victory of time as a prison. The human situation itself, pulled between consciousness of an ineffaceable existence and fixation in time, is radically dissatisfied. Death no longer appears as an "accident," but as an irrepressible question without answer, as an emptiness, as an ultimate "lack." In the "human cry," the universe, in its solidarity, calls out dramatically.

This refers us to one of St. Paul's very curious texts (Rom. 8, 19-24): "For the creation waits with eager longing for the revealing of the sons of God; for the creation was subjected to futility, not of its own will but by the will of him who subjected it in hope; because the creation itself will be set free from its bondage to decay and obtain the glorious liberty of the children of God. We know that the whole creation has been groaning in travail together until now; and not only the creation, but we ourselves, who have the first fruits of the Spirit, groan inwardly as we wait for adoption as sons, the redemption of our bodies."

These few sentences, written toward the end of the 1st century, sound strangely "modern." The solidarity of the real universe—corporeal and living—with the human race is expressed in them with rare force 1,900 years before it became an affirmation of the most advanced sciences. The

dynamic tension, the human "contradiction" ("he who subjected creation to futility" is evidently "man," which will bring
us to reflect later on the idea of "sin" which "introduces
death"), the drama of liberation, are underlined here as an
aspect of this solidarity, but as the truly capital aspect.

Like Isaiah, Paul uses the idea of giving birth, not as a
vague image, but as the strongest and most adequate expression to convey what he means.

Giving birth. In other words, this text refers us to the
very complex and fundamental world of sexuality. It seems to
me that we can reflect on the *real* phenomenon of death only
according to a first, and then implicitly continued, reference
to sexuality as the specific structure of life.

Except for the most elementary protozoa, sexual organization appears on the level of the most primitive living beings,
and its specificity and complexity become increasingly precise,
to the degree that the living organism is perfected. Its principle
is very simple: since the heliozoa, in each species two individuals that are similar, but structured differently and comple-
mentarily in an area of their constitution, come together in a
conjunction whose modalities are very diverse, to give rise to
new individuals at the very beginning of their development.
Therefore, except for the very first monocellular "outlines,"
sexual organization is the mode of perpetuation of the particular form of living structure which a species represents.

But at the same time, it reveals the fundamental law of
living structure: the individual as such grows old and dies.
The amoeba reproduces by scission, and so we could not
perceive this law on its level. But from the very primitive level
where reproduction is sexual, it appears; individuals continue
with their own proper structure after reproduction, and so this
fundamental law of aging and death manifests itself clearly.
From the foraminifers to the human species, sexuality is at the
same time apparently an indefinite perpetuation of specific
forms of life *and* unequivocal revelation of the mortality *of the
individual*. Without pushing this to the paradoxical, we can

say that, despite everything, there is a kind of unexplainable dialectical tension.

The discussion with the Sadducees turns around marriage —that is, sexuality in its human expression. Christ specifies that in the world of the resurrection which he is establishing in power from that time on—realistic and not mythical resurrection—sexuality is infinitely *surpassed as a function.* We can situate this strange affirmation better by referring to the totality of what it reveals. It is not a question of *explaining* it, but of *situating* it *better;* the difference is important.

If we look upon human sexuality as the expression of something else much vaster than itself and than the function of reproduction (at least in the couple's success!), we can translate the essential by saying that the human race— *conscious* experience of living structure—has the dynamic rhythm of "two which tend to one" (without attaining it, however). This "one," which the couple is, gives rise to a "third." But the latter, in turn, is sexual—that is, he is fundamentally and inexorably inscribed in the constitutional duality of the living world.

But if we accept the perspectives of biblical revelation, we notice that "God"—the "I exist" of Exodus, inaccessible and very near, unimaginable and interior, outside the reach of every mythical representation—reveals himself as subsistent love, if we may use the expression, and as the transcendent and absolute unity of three absolutely distinct *persons.* This situates us *infinitely beyond the sexual,* and beyond any possibility of adequate expression. And Christ's revelation is that by death and resurrection with him, we enter "by adoption" into this "trinitary system" which is the "life of God."

In this perspective, death is nothing but an aspect of sexual structure; we might say that it is a "moment" in which creation, which began an experiment—ambivalent and unsuccessful, or rather, insufficient—of love, passes from this stage of time to eternal existence, properly speaking, escaping from the prison of the "two" to accede to the "three and one," beyond the limits of this first structure, by a real rupture which thrusts the creature beyond the prison of his limitations by means of the all-powerful dynamism of love.

Thus we have sexuality as the revelation of death, and the Word of God completes it: as a surpassing, a liberation from *insufficiency,* and access to the inconceivable world of *perfect* love. This implies that the sexuated—and sexual—mode of the relation is not an "error" or an "evil," but an *insufficiency.* And this clarifies in a singular way the fact that death and sexuality are so profoundly connected in observable reality.

In this way—and only in this way—can we justify the psychologically and physiologically possible decision of those men and women who choose to live, even in time, "beyond the sexual" in religious celibacy.

In the Christian concept of man, it is clear that the idea of death is also connected to that of "sin." But this term is very equivocal because it has moralistic connotations in modern language, and it therefore requires a few reflections.

Contamination by Platonic and Stoic currents of thought, among others, has undoubtedly conditioned theological reflection strongly, up to modern times. There is nothing surprising or shocking in this, since reflection did not yet have scientific knowledge, properly speaking, at its disposal and it needed conceptual and verbal material in order to express itself. But now it is necessary to distinguish, and not attribute to revelation what really results from a mythological sort of Greek "cosmology."

Expressions like "the original fall" and "fallen man" cannot be found in the Bible, which expresses the human drama in a different way, in a dialogue with someone, and as a drama of love. In like manner, it is not mentioned explicitly in the first three chapters of Genesis that man is "created immortal." In fact, in the second creation narrative (Gen. 2, 17), man is told (before the appearance of woman) that if he should "eat of the fruit of the tree of knowledge, he will surely die"— a strange sentence. The creation of the couple is not yet completed (whereas, in the first narrative, this creation is simultaneous and indissociable). It seems that the accent is placed in a primordial way on the fact that, by his fault of pride, man is confronted painfuly and inexorably with his contradiction of being in duration (that is, in death).

However, this reminds us of St. Paul's words (Rom. 5, 12): "Therefore as sin came into the world through one man and death through sin. . . ." First of all, this sentence must be situated in its context. The apostle is balancing the one who introduced sin with Christ who came to save us. The accent is placed on human unity, and nothing can express it more distinctly in the culture of that time than the unicity of a "personage."

Then, too, it is quite clear in the general context of his letter that when Paul speaks of death, he is not referring to the clinical fact of biological death, as our modern scientific mentality would tend to make us think. He is speaking of the death which is "separation from God," of "spiritual" death, as the note in the Jerusalem Bible emphasizes.

This helps very much to put a modern mind at ease, a mind more or less penetrated by scientific knowledge. The idea of a "primitive time" in which human beings were not mortal is really shocking. But this idea *is not biblical,* or even Semitic; it comes from Greek philosophy and mythology. In fact, if we look at the biblical text closely, we see that what "sin," the "inaugural"attitude of human liberty in its signification of rupture, introduces is not explicitly death as such, but rather *suffering.*

This attitude is a refusal to hear the Word of the other. Yahweh demands that his creature respect his *actual* limits, that he not try to surpass them, and therefore that he have total confidence in God. This proves that the creature in question can be tempted—in other words, that he is both limited and "desirous" beyond these limits, capable of conceiving of a beyond confusedly, without which no question could be posed.

This is the classic and crucial problem of liberty. But in modern anthropology, it appears that this conflict of liberty and this contradictory tension are much more fundamental and intrinsic than we could express them up until now. What we call, traditionally but very equivocally, "original sin" is much more central and much more real than we could imagine. But we can no longer represent it with the image of the disobedience of a subordinate to his superior; this representation, which conditions habitual language, has become insufficient to express such a central and deeply mysterious reality.

Freud's discoveries have introduced us to a knowledge of this ambivalence which we mentioned in a preceding chapter. In a way unimagined until then, it places our finger on the very crux of our contradictory obscurity. The "death drives" are not an "accident" in human nature; they are an aspect of it. (Can we perhaps see a lived translation of this fact in that a human being is unsatisfied with his limitation in the consciousness-duration contradiction?)

In what does this mystery consist? We must avoid any "concordism" here. All that we can do is situate it better; we cannot clarify it, because it escapes our grasp by its very essence. On the anthropological side, we ascertain that death is a normal biological rhythm for the individual, that it is lived by us in an ambivalent way, that consciousness perceives itself as indestructible, and that we spend our time wanting to arrest life by somehow denying duration in duration itself.

On the revealed side, we hear someone who is love and who loves us. This someone is beyond duration, and he asks us to live unhurriedly in our situation while placing our confidence in him unhesitatingly. But we do not listen to him, and we confuse our desire for non-duration, which we cannot experience, with our duration itself. Death then appears as failure, a "black hole," the inexorable catastrophe, and finally the place where someone comes to look for us himself, because his love has asserted itself from the beginning as being without limit and without "withdrawal."[1]

---

[1] But between the anthropological side and the revealed side, there is—if I may say so!—the inaccessible crest of transcendence. Neither "proves" the other.

A comparison can clarify somewhat this aspect which seems to be fundamental. I live in an apartment on the second floor; I "install" myself in it, and I form my habits. But the landlord has rented it to me only temporarily, because in a few years he will give me the apartment on the third floor, with which I am not acquainted and which I have never entered, but which I know is much more spacious, pleasing, comfortable and rent-free. In spite of myself, my reaction will be to forget that the first lodgings are temporary; it is inevitable, because I have to live in the meantime. A person has to organize himself to live; and it does us no good to say that it is only for a time, because we nevertheless organize ourselves so that each night we find our chair under our lamp at the place where we like it and in a position we have chosen. And when the time comes to leave the first for the second, two things will happen: it will be hard for me to *tear myself* from what I know, and I will be irritated to have to be indebted to my landlord from now on, even though I know that it is a pure act of generosity on his part and that he asks nothing of me but that I accept it. To overcome these two things, he himself will have to come to help me to move.

Everything happens as if there were in me a force of adherence to the immediacy of duration which contradicts my expectation of the "definitive"—my desire not to be the landlord's slave. "Original sin" is nothing but this strange contradiction, this distrust, this demand of false independence, which makes us hold tight to the armchair and slippers of life in time as if they were the source of non-duration.

The passage from time to non-time—which, according to biblical revelation, is our destiny—is therefore conflict with this someone (conflict in which we are *culpable* of refusing love), but it is also agony and suffering, just like all existence in time which prepares it.

Sometimes a false problem is posed: "And if there had not been any original sin, what would have happened?" St. Thomas Aquinas himself remarks that it is stupid to pose false problems, and especially this one. "Original sin" perhaps consists in posing false problems to give ourselves the illusion of having thrown off what surpasses us.

But in order to understand better the meaning of death in the Christian vision of the world, can't we say that, without this unexplainable aspect in the conflict of liberty, we would pass from duration to beyond duration without shock, without tearing, without reticence or uprooting? This is undoubtedly the profound meaning of what the Church affirms with regard to Mary, the Virgin Mother of Jesus, when it speaks of her "assumption."

It is interesting to ascertain that sensation and suffering can be dissociated. Certain drugs or surgical interventions on the brain can end up in this very paradoxical result: a cancer patient who cannot be operated upon continues to feel the same "pains," but they no longer make him "suffer"; he no longer feels *bad* although he is feeling the same things. He will continue to say, for example, "It is as though a fox were gnawing at my liver," but he will say it smiling and without suffering. And it is not *theoretically* inconceivable that death might be lived and felt in the same way.

In these perspectives, the difficult question concerning the "origins of man" becomes quite secondary. From the viewpoint we are discussing, wouldn't this be another false problem? Paleontology and pre-history are far from discovering the human race's point of emergence. Did a mutation take place in a single couple? Did a mutation take place simultaneously among many scattered groups? Without doubt, it would be harmful to retain a mentality like Bossuet's on this point. The inaugural biblical affirmation has neither paleontological value nor paleontological consequence in the actual sense of the term; its signification is of an entirely different order, much more profound and much more important for the comprehension of our destiny. To express the profound, revealed sense of the human drama, the Semitic mentality of the second millennium before Christ had at its disposal neither the knowledge nor the vision of the world which we have. People lived in a tribal and patriarchal world, and nothing could be expressed except in this unique way. Even the representation of Yahweh in Genesis 3 is strongly colored. Nor could they conceive of human history except in this mode, and this resulted in the image of the first man, who was, nevertheless and strangely enough, designated by the collective word. But that is not the central idea of the text; it is not the mythical form which is proposed to us as the Word of God, but rather the idea-force for which it serves as a vehicle: human liberty's drama of "rupture" makes death a tearing apart and a prison, which cannot be separated from it or broken except by God's own irruption into the drama.

The evolutionist's vision of the universe is recent. It was made possible by the discoveries of the natural sciences, of pre-history, and of that individual pre-history that is psychoanalysis.

Likewise, the unitary vision of the human being, joining, basically, with the spirit of hylomorphism as St. Thomas developed it, breaks with the body-soul dualism which has conditioned practically all of language during the last several centuries. This results in the fact that the scientific vision of man and of the universe is a totalitarian vision, independent of any theological or philosophical preliminaries. The Christian vision of man is also totalitarian. But it is of another order than scientific. The latter terminates with death as a question. The former includes death as an event which is both dramatic and a completion.

Language and Resurrection

According to the most ancient and most authentic Christian tradition, death is therefore Christ's entrance into the world of fullest and most realistic existence, that of the "resurrection of the body." I think that we must understand by this word "body" man's psychosomatic condition as such, in time, taken in this dramatic contradiction of "original sin."

But how can we speak of this "world of the resurrection"?

This is undoubtedly one of the most irritating stumbling blocks in language. We are concerned at the very depths and in the very center of ourselves, and yet we quickly realize that everything which we try to say about it is ridiculously inadequate and even puerile.

A "stupid question" presents itself. If, since the time that men first appeared on earth and began to die, everyone resurrected with his body, how could there possibly be enough space for these billions and billions of people without their suffocating or walking on one another's feet? Such a question manifests our absolute incapability to form phantasms or images of it—that is, to even attempt to comprehend it in our temporal mode of knowing. The world of the resurrection is one which, by definition, absolutely escapes duration and, therefore, this mode of knowing. Consequently, we really *cannot say anything*.

Any imagining, as soon as we lose its sense of purely symbolic signification and total insufficiency, quickly becomes an affliction. Origen, who subscribed to the neo-Platonic vision of things, held a pseudo-reasoning which was rigorous but in which the impossibility of disengaging oneself from the imaginary appears: "Perfection is the circle or sphere; bodies in glory are perfect; therefore, they are spherical." And this solves every problem for him.

However, it does seem that knowledge acquired by biology furnishes us with a line of reflection which somehow enables us not to speak of the world of the resurrection, but to understand better how and why we are unable to speak of it, and therefore to situate it more satisfactorily as real and inexpressible. It is what we might call the analogy with birth. The foetus that moves during the last month of pregnancy is already virtually an individual personality in potency—in other words, an affective reaction whose existence as well as its confused obscurity has been shown to us by modern psychology. Someone's history is already beginning.

I was already "I," obscurely, before I was born. It is evidently impossible for me to speak adequately of what "happened for me" at that time. But in the drama that is lived at birth and in its ambivalence, psychoanalysis has discovered certain elements which enable us to reflect on it strangely enough and to speak of it in an analogical way.

At this primitive time of my existence, I was at ease in a closed world. Everything was brought to me without any effort on my part by a "surrounding world" whose nature I could not suspect. I was closed in on myself, in the amniotic pocket which was part of my distinct biological being. But already there was within me, by the very law of life, what I might call "the desire for something else," the "need to get out," which my first attempts at what would be successful gestures in the future expressed visibly. But at the same time, the reactions which follow birth show that there existed in me also this "satisfaction with a passive comfort," which was contradictory and already establishing an ambivalence. The "desire to return to the maternal womb," the agony to which it gives rise, and the affective evolution which takes place within this conflict itself are the undebatable signs of it.

When I was within my mother's womb, without *yet knowing* it, I was already divided between adherence to the immediate and dissatisfaction with this temporary situation. My "relation to the other person" was very limited; and to "know" —to become truly myself—it was necessary that, according to the very dynamism of life, with an unexplorable active participation by myself, I separate myself from part of myself, tear myself out of my wrappings, go out of my mother, open my eyes, and progressively *see* the exterior.

Before my birth, I existed in a proteiform situation, but in a sense already comparable to my situation in conscious existence in time: desiring to "see" something else, but without being able to obtain *the least idea* of what it could be. And to begin to see, I had to "die" to intra-uterine life. Obviously, I have not "finished," as is well shown by the consciousness-duration dialectic which is at the very base of human uneasiness.

And so, if my birth was a "death which made me live," why

couldn't my death be the second stage of my birth which will make me live "for good"? And just as I "adhered" to my intra-uterine existence to the point that my birth *was a drama,* I "adhere to life in time" to the point that I *suffer* and that death also is a drama.[2]

But, eight days before my birth, I was absolutely incapable of "knowing" what I was going to discover. Likewise, in life in time, I am absolutely incapable of knowing what death will bring me to discover. At most, I can vaguely hope that it will be the perfection of love, without my being able to represent to myself in any way in what this can consist.

Just as, at the time, nothing permitted me to evoke an image of my father, *who nevertheless had put me there,* if I may say so, so also, during the course of time, nothing permits me to imagine in any way him "who has put us here." The only point of reference is, exactly, Christ dead *and resurrected.* But although it is accessible from a certain historical approach and by means of faith in it, the other side of the event remains as analogically unexplorable as my parents' room was to me when my mother felt her first labor pains which led to my birth.

However, this comparison with birth is far from being a new one. In the first centuries of Christianity, when the anniversary of a martyr's death was celebrated, they spoke of the *dies natalis*—the day of birth, understood definitively.

We find the origin of this very explicit idea in Jesus' conversation with Nicodemus in Chapter 3 of the gospel according to St. John. This unsatisfied Pharisee was intrigued by Jesus; he had a feeling that Jesus had the truth, and that the Jewish expectation was perhaps about to be realized. Clandestinely ("at night," undoubtedly, for fear that his colleagues might make an issue of it), he came to find Jesus, and he questioned him concerning the "kingdom" which he was announcing.

---

[2] It is quite evident that this is only a manner of speaking, or, more precisely, a comparison offered. Biologically, the foetus' continuity with its nurse does not correspond to the biological "rupture" of death. But from the viewpoint of the "I," the comparison is a suggestive one.

Jesus' answer was very clear: "Unless a man be born again" (or "from on high," according to a translation which is perhaps more exact, but which does not exclude the idea of a second stage.), "he cannot enter the kingdom of God."

Nicodemus' reaction is very significant; he thinks this means that a man must reenter his mother's womb. This idea of "return to the maternal womb," whose importance from the very beginning of affective life has been underlined by psychoanalysis, is an old idea; among some peoples, the dead are buried in a foetal position. But Jesus tries to make him understand that this is not what he meant; rather, he means what we might call a new birth "forward", to "be born of water and of the Spirit" (which announces the sign of baptism). Death is not return to the maternal womb; it is entrance into definitive life, *eternal,* properly speaking. It is evident that this perspective agrees better with what modern psychology has discovered of the dialectic of agony and of sublimation *in the technical sense of this term.*

Faith in Christ is not a "mystery religion"; it is the most realistic perspective there is of a completion of the *person* in a mode of being which totally surpasses the power of imagination. In fact, this is what causes the difficulty.

The strange thing is that in the first centuries, as all of the documents substantiate, Christians had a sharp and ever present consciousness of this "birth" aspect of death, but this consciousness slowly disappeared, to the point that we no longer speak about it, and we forget that it is essential to faith in Christ. Temporalistic illusions concerning the kingdom of heaven are probably responsible for this.

It is not paradoxical to say that modern anthropology, centered as it is around the Freudian discoveries and the world which they opened up, as it leads us to a more methodical consciousness of the uncomfortable and insoluble ambivalence of the human condition, enables Christian thought to purify itself and to progress on its own level, which is of an absolutely other order.

How the Christian Vision Is Lived

In his letter to the Christians of Rome, St. Paul wrote, "Do you not know that all of us who have been baptized into Christ Jesus were baptized into his death? We were buried therefore with him by baptism into death, so that as Christ was raised from the dead by the glory of the Father, we too might walk in newness of life. For if we have been united with him in a death like his, we shall certainly be united with him in a resurrection like his. We know that our old self was crucified with him so that the sinful body might be destroyed, and we might no longer be enslaved to sin. For he who has died is freed from sin. But if we have died with Christ, we believe that we shall also live with him. For we know that Christ being raised from the dead will never die again; death no longer has dominion over him. The death he died he died to sin, once for all, but the life he lives he lives to God. So you also must consider yourselves dead to sin and alive to God in Christ Jesus" (Rom. 6, 3-11).

"He who has died is freed from sin." This strange sentence must be situated in context with other expressions of Paul; it returns to the idea that there is a relation between time and what Paul calls "sin." This same term, "sin," recurs in the same epistle in a surprising expression: "If I do the evil which I do not want, it is no longer I that do it, but sin which dwells within me."

The mysterious reality is present in man who imprisons himself in his bodily condition (the "flesh" which is opposed to the "Spirit")—that is, in his *duration* and in the illusion that this duration can, *by itself,* end up beyond itself, the mysterious and dramatic situation of the man who refuses to hear the Word of this other who is love, this other who is both transcendent and intimately present at the very heart of the human question.

Death in Christ, therefore, delivers from time which, instead of being a stage, has been made a prison by "sin," from death, lived as a brutal rupture, tearing, and break, like birth and childbirth (even so-called "painless" childbirth). The "in pain you shall bring forth children" is of undoubtedly much greater consequence than we might believe at first sight.

This puts the man who *believes in Christ* in a situation that is simultaneously exalting and radically uncomfortable—a situation of *voyage*. On the Word of Christ in which he believes (the very center of Jesus' message is that we *believe in him*), he knows that he is going toward a bursting of the dialectic of time, toward the full existence of his *person* beyond duration, by the completion of divine adoption. (The strong meaning of the Preface in the Liturgy of the Dead is particularly striking on this point.) But he cannot form the least idea of what this represents with regard to the lived.

Therefore, he has to be present *simultaneously* to duration, the "things of time," and to the beyond duration—that is, what we call eternal life. Basically, this is the final point of all moral effort—to be present to the exigencies of time, and not to be their slave or prisoner, to give oneself entirely to the development of a better world in time, *and* to give oneself entirely to death, the necessary break which is a completion. Beginning in time, we must construct, at the price of one's own life, a world of love and of justice, *and* at the same time prepare the definitive birth of death "in Christ," as St. Paul says, by means of renunciations and successive purifications.

We conceive without difficulty that this is at the same time very easy in intention ("I can will what is right," says St. Paul) and dramatically difficult to carry out daily ("but I cannot do it"). It is consciousness of this drama which enables us to *hear* the Word of him who says, "He who believes in me, he who eats my flesh and drinks my blood has eternal life, and I will raise him up on the last day." As St. Paul says in the letter to the Romans, "Who will deliver me from this body of death? Thanks be to God through Jesus Christ our Lord!"

This sums up the *Christian* sense of death, and goes as far as reflection will go.

It is striking to note that human thought, no matter how

spontaneous or elaborate it is, impulsively tends toward a scotoma—that is, a central evacuation, an attitude of *not seeing*—and what we "do not see" are sexuality and death. Perhaps we joke about them and "make up sayings", or we speak and think as though there were no question of them. Angelism and idealism are closely connected, as everyone knows—that is, the tendency to forget that we are sexuated and mortal, in this perspective, nevertheless real and evident, of the consciousness-duration dialectic which corresponds to what we call "original sin."

Without noticing it, some "moralizing moralists," according to Dr. Berge's expression in *Les maladies de la vertu,* reason as if the observance of precepts on their different levels *sufficed* to bring us to the "fullness of good," to the "last end." This is forgetfulness of the drama; it is the very opposite of what Christ's message and Paul's explanation teach us.

This idealist scotoma—which corresponds to a transitory aspect of the adolescent psychological crisis—is a defense against an unexplorable agony. Without any doubt, it also conditions what we might call Marxist idealism in the proper sense of the term: the impossibility, affective as well as rational, of assuming the positive signification of the "failure" of duration. And this agony is such that it requires an infinite respect to answer it in the name of Christ!

Some "theologians" run the danger of this evasion into the intellectual, which actually translates the same agony. Now and then, the Church's consciousness has expressed itself in the "condemnation" of opposite errors: Pelagians, Montanists, Jansenists, Quietists, etc. Isn't our modern world, with the radical newness of scientific knowledge (psychoanalysis included), better prepared than any other to develop what we might call a "theology of death" by taking account more methodically of what the "real" is?

Certain equivocations in language cannot help but occur. This is the case of some formulations, like those in the "Our Father." At first sight, they give us the impression of a very childish naiveté. We ask of God to be "freed from sin" and to be "preserved from all evil." "Freed from sin": if we understand by this that by the divine mercy "from now on and forever" we will commit no more faults, we are cheapening the very mystery of liberty and losing ourselves in the illusion of a total perfection whose impossibility, St. Paul tells us precisely, is the very place of encounter with Christ. What Christ frees us from is "sin" in the fundamental sense of the word, in the sense of the mystery of our own contradiction which St. Paul recalls so forcefully in his letter.

"Preserved from all evil": here, too, realism is necessary. Without it, we lend ourselves to the ridiculous or to scandal. Asking God that we have no more serious annoyances, sicknesses or any other kind of "evil" is a totemistic attitude which makes people laugh. But it can also give rise to a real scandal: despite prayer, "evils" come, and faith, when it is of a totemistic order, is also contradicted. We often hear someone in mourning say, "But what did I do to God for him to take him away from me?"—or make recriminations against this God who "leaves us and forgets us," as though it were not *natural* to die, and as though the conflict, drama and suffering were not *in fact* the human condition in time.

What this prayer asks for in a realistically Christian perspective, is to be preserved from being *crushed* by difficulties which will come, and to know how to put evils in their place: the signs of time which proceeds, the "pains of childbirth" of which St. Paul speaks.

There must be "evils" in existence, because there cannot really not be death, which is definitely the most evident and the most ambivalent of them. What counts is that we assume them when they present themselves, in order to progress in the discovery of the non-perceptible, instead of letting ourselves slide negatively into their traps. This is what we are really praying for in this prayer. But this does not dispense us from training ourselves, day after day, not to do evil to others.

One of Jesus' expressions, announcing that he would be put to death, is particularly striking: "If the seed does not die

. . . it remains alone." The image is evidently that of fecundity: the seed that "dies" in the soil will produce a multitude of seeds. The sciences of nature change the sense of this comparison a little, for everyone knows that the seed, in fact, does not *die,* but rather *begins to live*—that is, to germinate in a prodigious process of cellular proliferation. "If the seed dies, it bears much fruit"—but, also, it "is not alone."

When I was still in the warm obscurity of the maternal uterus, I was turned in on myself in a comfortable passivity, but I was *alone.* When I was born, I saw the light of day, according to the popular expression, (not immediately, but soon after) and little by little I knew "others," which enabled me to know myself. But something of this original ambivalence deeply persists—an unsurpassable opacity of relation, an insufficiency which results in the fact that, in exchanges, I can only give what *I have,* and not what *I am.* And sometimes I am still very *alone* in the impossibility of communicating totally. Then I "fall to the ground," I die to time, and I germinate in the unknowable of the promise. Finally, the remains of solitude will be dissipated, and truly I "will be with."

* * *

It seems to me that the ending of these pages, which are only a given stage in a process of reflection, should not be philosophical elaboration, but rather a thought committed personally to the most concrete of existence—and this as much for the author as for the reader.

The latter will not be shocked if I need to say now, with greater lucidity than when I began:

I *believe* in Christ dead and resurrected.
I *believe* in the resurrection of the body.
I *believe* in eternal life.